Martin Luther in Wittenberg
A Biographical Tour

D1246554

116

Martin Luther in Wittenberg
A Biographical Tour

by Martin Treu

Wittenberg 2003

"Martin Luther: Life – Work – Legacy" Permanent Exhibition in the Luther House in Wittenberg

Exhibition project team: Dr. Volkmar Joestel,
  Rosemarie Knape, Jutta Strehle, Dr. Martin Treu (coordinator)
Advisory board: Frieder Aechtner,
  Prof. Dr. Ulrich Barth, Prof. Dr. Helmar Junghans,
  Prof. Dr. Bernd Moeller, Prof. Dr. Dr. Johannes Schilling (chair),
  Günter Schuchardt, Gotthard Voß
Restoration: Karin Lubitzsch
Exhibition design: Gössel und Partner, Bremen
Direction: Dr. Stefan Rhein

Funded by:
The European Union (European Fund for Regional Development–EFRD)
The Federal Republic of Germany (Commissioner for Culture and Media)
The State of Saxony-Anhalt (Ministry of Education and Cultural Affairs)
The Protestant Church in Germany
Landesmarketing Sachsen-Anhalt GmbH

Cover design: Konstantin Zigmann
Editor: Rosemarie Knape
Catalog: Petra Wittig
Translation: Tradukas GbR
Production: LEWERENZ Medien+Druck GmbH

ISBN: 3-9808619-4-5

page

Preliminary Note

When the museum on the history of the Reformation was established in the former Black Cloister of the Hermits of St. Augustine in 1883, it bore the slightly obscure name Lutherhalle. Although the name above all reflected the spirit of the time, it overcame all resistance and gradually took hold. While preparing to reorganize the exhibition in 2002 it was decided, partly on the initiative of the advisory board, to change this to Luther House–a name that, it was felt, would more clearly express what this unique place in Wittenberg is all about. It is about Martin Luther, for the man and his work are inseparably linked to this house.

The exhibition "Martin Luther in Wittenberg–A Biographical Tour" aims to give visitors a first glimpse of the rooms and collections of the Luther House by illustrating a particular period in Luther's life. A complete biography or even a history of Protestantism in sixteenth-century Germany is beyond its scope. However, we would at this point like to draw attention to the other parts of the exhibition: "Luther's family life," "Preaching, Propaganda, Polemics – The Reformation as a Media Revolution," "Luther's Image and Images of Luther–Reception and Influence 1546–1983," "The Treasure Chamber–Precious Objects from Nine Centuries." These enable visitors with more time to gain a more comprehensive picture.

*"Come to Wittenberg, . . . whose citizens are well educa-
ted and men are devoted to the sciences."*

Christoph Scheurl, 1507

Martin Luther's Path to Wittenberg, 1483–1508

Martin Luther was no native of Wittenberg, even though
he was to spend most of his life in this town. He was born
on November 10, 1483 in Eisleben, where his father had
found employment in copper-shale mining. The next day
the boy was christened Martin after the saint whose feast
day it was on November 11. The house where Luther was
born is today a museum.

Shortly after the birth of their first son, the family moved
to Mansfeld. In the years to follow, the father rose from a
lowly worker to part-owner of mines and smelters. Hans
Luder (as the name was originally spelled) invested the
money he made in his son's education. At the age of five
the boy entered the local school and later continued his
education in Magdeburg and Eisenach.

In 1501 Martin Luther enrolled for liberal arts at the
famous University of Erfurt. His father clearly intended him
to become a lawyer. Luther concluded his studies in 1505
with a master's degree at the Faculty of Arts. Then his life
took an unexpected turn. On July 2, 1505, he was caught
in a thunderstorm at Stotternheim near Erfurt. Terrified by
bolts of lightning, he prayed: "Help me, St. Anne, I will
become a monk!" On July 17 he entered the order of the
Augustinian monks. After one year of probation he took
his solemn vows in September 1506.

The statue of St. Anne (Fig. 1 ▶) recalls this profound
change in Luther's life. What exactly moved him to enter
the monastery is not known, but it took his father a long
time to forgive him.

In 1507 Luther was ordained to the priesthood and in
accordance with the wishes of his superiors began to
study theology in the monastery. The devout young man
must have been exceptionally gifted, for by no means all
monks became priests or even studied theology. In retro-
spect Luther painted a gloomy picture of his Erfurt years.

■ *Fig. 1   St. Anne, Swabia, carved limewood, c. 1520*

Late in 1508, the founding dean of the Faculty of Theology of the University of Wittenberg, which had only been established in 1502, called Luther to Wittenberg to give lectures in moral philosophy while continuing his theological studies. After a brief interlude in Erfurt, Luther returned to Wittenberg for good in the fall of 1511 to prepare for his doctorate.

■ *Plate 1   View of Wittenberg, three-block woodcut, 1536–46*

Wittenberg – University Town and Electoral Residence

First mentioned in 1180, Wittenberg received a city charter in 1293. With around two thousand inhabitants, it was one of the medium-sized towns of the early sixteenth century. Luther had previously lived in Erfurt, which in contrast had around twenty thousand inhabitants. In the wake of the division instituted through the Treaty of Leipzig in 1485, *Prince Elector Frederick III of Saxony (Fig. 2)* had moved his residence to Wittenberg. One of the oldest *views of the town, dating from before 1546, illustrates the rapid and far-reaching changes in the townscape that ensued* (◄ *Plate 1, pp. 11–12):* The city's fortifications were rebuilt and reinforced. The elector assisted the Augustinians to build a new monastery in the eastern part of the town. Its name, the Black Cloister, refers to the color of the Augustinian habit. Adjoining it was the complex of the new university. In the west a Renaissance palace was erected whose north wing was taken up by the new Church of All Saints. The woodcut impressively shows the rays of the rising sun illuminating the monastery in which Martin Luther was to live and work.

■ *Fig. 2   Prince Elector Frederick III, Lucas Cranach the Elder (workshop), oil on wood, 1532*

A *modern model of the city* gives an overview of the community's structure. At its core is the City Church with the adjoining marketplace and the Town Hall as the meeting place of the emerging class of property-owning citizens.

Prince Elector Frederick of Saxony, dubbed "the Wise" even in his lifetime, drew substantial profits from silver mines in the Erzgebirge mountains. These funds financed a building boom that altered the face of the city between 1490 and 1525. At the same time, this Renaissance prince enjoyed sumptuous festivities and tournaments, for example a *joust (Fig. 3)* held in Wittenberg's marketplace in 1506.

■ *Fig. 3   Joust, Lucas Cranach the Elder, woodcut, 1506, private loan*

The author of the woodcut, Lucas Cranach the Elder, had been appointed Frederick's court painter shortly beforehand. One of his tasks was to document such pageants, which increased a reigning prince's prestige.

Another of Cranach's tasks was to illustrate a catalog of the many relics in the possession of Frederick the Wise, the *Wittenberger Heiltumsbuch (Wittenberg Book of Relics)* compiled in 1509 *(Fig. 4)*.

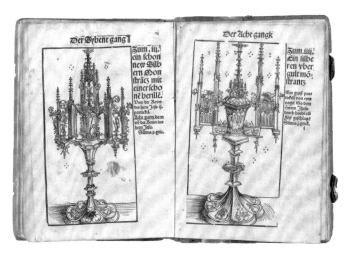

■ *Fig. 4* *Double page showing reliquaries, Lucas Cranach the Elder, from Lucas Cranach the Elder's Wittenberg Book of Relics (Wittenberg: Symphorian Reinhart, 1509), on loan from the State of Saxony-Anhalt*

The prince elector was a great collector of relics. In 1509 he already owned 5,005 of them, including several vials of the milk of the Virgin Mary, straw from the manger, and the entire corpse of one of the innocents massacred by King Herod. The relics were kept in reliquaries–artistically wrought vessels mostly of silver gilt–and exhibited once a year for the faithful to venerate. In 1509 each devout visitor who donated toward the preservation of the Castle Church (Schlosskirche) received an indulgence of one hundred days per relic.

In the following years the prince elector not only increased the number of relics to reach 19,013 in 1520, but also extended the indulgences related to them, so that finally the faithful could reduce their stay in purgatory by up to 1.9 million years. This quantification of piety is typical of pre-Reformation conditions.

The veneration of relics went hand in hand with a deep-felt veneration of the saints. *St. Anthony of the Desert (Fig. 5 ▶)* was especially popular with the citizens of Wittenberg. The Egyptian saint was regarded as the founder of Christian monasticism. The religious order founded in 1095 that venerated him as their patron saint also had a house in Wittenberg. According to tradition,

■ *Fig. 5* *St. Anthony, Lucas Cranach the Elder (workshop), oil on wood, c. 1520, on loan from the State of Saxony-Anhalt, excerpt*

Anthony's sole companion in the desert was a pig, and he was depicted in art accompanied by this animal. Just as their brethren elsewhere, Wittenberg's monks of St. Anthony held the privilege of keeping swine. The townspeople fed the pigs, an act that was considered pious. To distinguish them from their worldly cousins, the order's pigs wore small bells in their ears and had a St. Anthony's cross shaved into the bristles on their backs.

■ *Fig. 6   St. Sebastian, Lucas Cranach the Elder (workshop), oil on wood, c. 1520, on loan from the State of Saxony-Anhalt, excerpt*

In 1513 the incensed prince elector forbade the Wittenberg townspeople to deck out their pigs in a similar style to dupe their neighbors into feeding them.

Another saint popular in Wittenberg was *Sebastian* (*Fig. 6*). Tradition makes him a captain of Diocletian's guard who helped prisoners during the persecution of the Christians. In punishment he was tied to a tree and shot with arrows. In the Middle Ages he was one of the saints whose intervention people prayed for in the epidemics that intermittently swept Europe. In Wittenberg he was the patron saint of the influential marksmen's association formed by the town's most important citizens. In 1412 they endowed a separate altar in the City Church (Stadtkirche) at which five masses were read each week. The size of both images suggests that they were probably meant for private prayer.

In addition to the Augustinian Hermits and the monks of St. Anthony, Franciscan monks also maintained a monastery in the city. Established in 1261, it housed the tomb of the ruling princes until Frederick III expanded the Castle Church. The Franciscan monastery was one of the first to fall victim to the Reformation. Standing empty since 1523, it was converted into a grain store in 1537. It must have been on this occasion that the *sandstone corbel* showing evidence of the influence of the Prague-based Parler school was salvaged.

Both the prince elector and the townspeople sought to prove their faith by endowing liturgical instruments. The

■ *Fig. 7   Disc candlestick, brass, sixteenth century*

prince was able to afford ninety-three chasubles for priests and thirty-three dalmatics for the deacons, all embroidered with gold and silver and ornamented with precious stones, to be used in his Collegiate Chapter of All Saints. The humble citizens made do with *brass candlesticks and censers (Fig. 7)*.

Little is known about Luther's views on the inflationary traits of late-medieval piety. Although he served the town as a priest from around 1514, he saw his main task as closely studying the Holy Scriptures. In particular, he consulted the Bible commentaries of early Christianity, and the *marginalia by his hand* in a volume of the works of St. Jerome edited by Erasmus of Rotterdam bear striking witness to this work. Jerome (347/48–420) lived in Palestine and translated the Bible from the original Hebrew of the Old Testament and Greek of the New Testament into Latin. He thus created the basis for the medieval Bible, called the Vulgate, the popular version. Luther returned to his writings at different times. The oldest marginalia, for which he used red ink, can be dated to the years 1516–17.

Admiration for the early Christian authors, who in contrast to the later scholastic theologians were regarded as authentic and pure, was something Luther shared with the "Prince of Humanists," Erasmus of Rotterdam. Luther, however, considered Augustine (354–430) a more important theologian than Jerome. Although he considered both to be outstanding exegetes – and that was his real interest – Luther felt that in contrast to Jerome, who was mainly preoccupied with linguistic issues, Augustine pointed the way to a theology that explored "the kernel of the nut and the marrow of the bone." Moreover, as a monk, Luther felt a close tie with the patron saint of his order.

"Where Christ is, there he always goes against the flow."
Martin Luther in a sermon held on February 2, 1517

Luther's Reformational Discovery

After taking his doctoral degree in 1512, Luther succeeded to the chair of biblical theology, which was traditio-
nally considered less important than philosophical theology. But Luther's lifelong calling was the exposition of the
Holy Scriptures, and it was for this reason that he began
to study the original languages of the Bible.

From 1513–18 Luther gave four lectures on individual
books of the Bible, beginning with Psalms. His discussion of St. Paul's Epistle to the Romans led him to suggest that Christians find salvation only by faith in God's
justice.

Events were to prove how revolutionary this seemingly
academic insight was. Emphasizing the divine gift of
grace in Christ made all human effort to acquire merit
meaningless: Christ alone would save the faithful. This
conviction is vividly evident in the greater-than-life depiction of *Christ on the Cross (Fig. 8)* by Lucas Cranach the
Younger. Luther himself in 1538 put it this way: "He who
takes to heart the words 'He that believeth in me' need
not fear the Last Judgment."

It is not quite clear when Luther's reading of the Epistle
to the Romans threw up this insight. We do know, however, that it occurred in his private study in the tower
whose foundations are today to be seen in the entrance
building. For the time being, he did not make his views
public. His lectures, which were only rediscovered in the
nineteenth century, were held behind the university walls.

Instead, he rose within the order, where he bore the
responsibilities of a sub-prior. He was appointed district
vicar in 1515 and supervised eleven Augustinian houses
in the area of Dresden, Magdeburg, Wittenberg, and
Erfurt. He traveled extensively to learn about conditions
there.

■ *Fig. 8   Christ on the Cross, Lucas Cranach the Younger, oil on
canvas, 1571, on loan from the Wittenberg Preachers
Seminary*

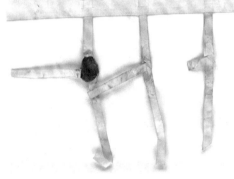

■ *Fig. 9* *Document on parchment on the sale of an annual tithe in the possession of the Monastery of the Hermits of St. Augustine in Wittenberg to the Collegiate Chapter of All Saints (Castle Church), Wittenberg, May 5, 1509*

The university of Wittenberg flourished at first, with 416 students enrolling in the term it was founded. Building an efficient administration, however, took its time. A *parchment (Fig. 9)* on the sale of an annual tithe in the possession of the monastery to the Collegiate Chapter of All Saints, dated May 5, 1509, was written by Johannes von Staupitz himself. Apparently, Luther's mentor, the vicar general to the observant Augustinian order, had no professional scribe.

The university's original *seal* showed St. Augustine with the translated motto "He that followeth me shall not walk in darkness" (John 8:12). From 1514 a *new seal* was used with the portrait of the elector, Frederick the Wise, and the motto "Under my reign Wittenberg began to teach." The older seal passed to the Faculty of Theology. This also indicates that changes were taking place within the university.

■ *Fig. 10   Luther with Doctoral Cap, Daniel Hopfer, etching, 1523*

An etching by Daniel Hopfer from the year 1523 depicts *Luther with his doctoral cap (Fig. 10)*, publicly documenting his claim to the title of "Sworn Doctor of the Holy Scriptures." Depiction in full profile was previously restricted to worldly and churchly dignitaries.

Johannes Tezelius Dominicaner Münch/ mit sei-
nen Römischen Ablaßkram/ welchen er im Jahr Christi 1517. in Deutschen-
landen zu marckt gebracht/ wie er in der Kirchen zu Pirn in seinem
Vaterland abgemahlet ist.

tschen mercket mich recht/
Des heiligen Vaters Papstes Knecht/
nd br in euch ist allein/
tausent vnd neun hundert car ein/
Ablaß von einer Sünd/
euch/ ewer Eltern/ Weib vnd Kind/
der gewehret sein
iel ihr legt ins Kästelein/
er Gülden im Becken klingt/
huy die Seel im Himel springt/

Babst Leo der zehend genandt/
Nu mehr fast vnmüglich befand/
as er das Römisch Jubel Jahr
ebet/ hat er die faule wahr/
blaßkrams in Deutschenland/
ch seine Kramknecht ausgesandt/
sich denn ohn all verdrieß/
ann Tetzel gebrauchen ließ/
as ist kaum dem Hencker entlauffen/
er wegen Ehebruchs solt ersauffen/
icht der from Fürst Friederich/
iner het angenommen sich/
eim Keyser Maximilian/
n gnedigste Fürbit gethan/
ey es aber so nicht blieb/
s ein Ehebrecher wurd ein Dieb/
r durch vermeint gewalt vnd macht/
el Gelds vnd Guts zu weg gebracht/

Als er die blinde Welt bered/
Das er den Himel feil tragen thet/
Wenn man nu Gelt gnug gebe dar/
Hets mit den Menschen kein gefahr/
So bald der Grosch im Kasten klingt/
So bald die Seel in Himel sich schwin
Durch diesen Teuffelischen Tande/
Hat er betrogen sein Vaterland/
Biß ihn Gott hat ins Spiel gesehen/
Durch Doctor Luthern seligen/
Welcher ihm seinen Krämertisch/
Gewaltiglich zu Boden stieß/
Daher/ Gott lob/ biß auff die zeit/
Der Ablaßkram zerstrewet leit/
So bleibet nun Christi verdienst/
Einig allein vnser Gewinst/
Des Tezels Kram vnd Bapsts Betrug/
Findet bey vns kein recht noch fug.

"The true treasure of the Church is the Most Holy Gospel of the glory and the grace of God."

Martin Luther in the sixty-second thesis, 1517

The Ninety-five Theses – the Beginnings of the Reformation, 1517

Indulgences emerged during the Middle Ages as a form of pecuniary penance by believers for their sins. Paying the costs of a pilgrimage to Rome could thus take the place of a pilgrimage itself. During the Renaissance, indulgences deteriorated into a means for the papacy to cover its ever-increasing financial needs. The indulgence for sale in the Archbishopric of Magdeburg from 1515, for example, served the ostensible purpose of financing the completion of St. Peter's Basilica in Rome. An *etching by Jakob Binck (Fig. 12)*, however, shows that the church was still not completed in the second half of the sixteenth century. In breach of an explicit ban issued by the pope, its parvis was even used as a venue for jousts.

■ *Fig. 12   The Great Joust, Jakob Binck, copperplate engraving, sixteenth century*

■ *Fig. 11   Caricature of Johann Tetzel selling indulgences, woodcut, 1617*

ALBERTVS· MI·DI·SA· SANC
ROMANE· ECCLAE· TI· SAN
CHRYSOGONI· PBR· CARDINA:
MAGVN· AC· MAGDE· ARCHI
EPS· ELECTOR· IMPE· PRIMAS
ADMINI· HALBER· MARCHI
BRANDENBVRGENSIS

SIC· OCVLOS· SIC· ILLE· GENAS· SIC
ORA· FEREBAT·
·ANNO· ETATIS· SVE· XXX·
·MD·XX·

■ *Fig. 13 Cardinal Albrecht of Brandenburg, Lucas Cranach the Elder, copperplate engraving, 1520*

In reality, the 1515 indulgence was intended to raise the money that Duke Albrecht of Brandenburg, *Archbishop of Magdeburg (Fig. 13)*, needed to pay the debts he had made with the Holy See in his bid for the Archbishopric of Mainz. Plurality of offices was prohibited, and moreover, church law stated that Albrecht was too young for his office. Special papal licenses had to be bought for several thousand florins. The powerful Fugger banking house in Augsburg gave the hopeful candidate a loan, and Albrecht commissioned one of the most brilliant salesmen of indulgences. Although the picture of *Johann Tetzel* (◄ *Fig. 11*) hails from a much later date (1617), it shows how popular he was in his time. He is depicted with foxtails in his hand, sitting on a donkey in front of an indulgence chest. Tetzel is also said to have coined the legendary phrase, "As soon as the gold in the casket rings, the rescued soul to heaven springs." Luther used it in a slightly varied form in his theses against indulgences. The money Tetzel collected was put into an *indulgence chest (Fig. 14)* that had at least three locks whose keys were in the custody of different persons, including representatives of the Fugger banking house and ecclesiastic notaries.

Pope Leo X (Fig. 15 ►) legitimized the campaign in a magnificent *document* similar to the one shown here, which was issued in 1492 by eighteen cardinals of the Salzburg diocese. For their money the faithful received a *letter of indulgence (Fig. 16 ►)*, a confessional letter that permitted them to make a complete confession once in their lifetime and at the hour of death, and gain absolution.

■ *Fig. 14   Indulgence chest, sheet iron bound with iron straps, wrought lid with five locks, sixteenth century*

■ *Fig. 15   Pope Leo X, Tobias Stimmer after Raphael, woodcut, 1573*

■ *Fig. 16   Letter of indulgence, parchment, with blanks, 1515*

The writ of indulgence to be seen in the exhibition is one of only five surviving writs of the St. Peter indulgence. It was printed on vellum to make it more durable. The text has blanks for the name of the purchaser and the amount to be contributed. The woodcut from the *title page of a Reformation pamphlet (Fig. 17)* gives an impression of the way indulgences were marketed.

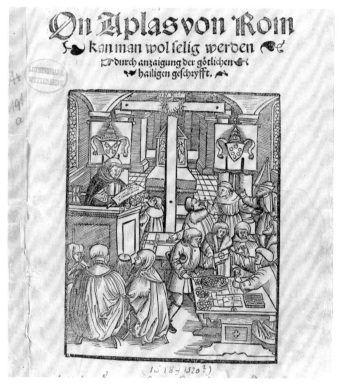

■ *Fig. 17   Traffic in indulgences, from Without Indulgence from Rome One Can Still be Saved (Augsburg: Melchior Ramminger, 1521)*

By his own words Martin Luther only learned of the issue of indulgences from his parishioners when in around 1514, as *monk and professor (Fig. 18 ▶)*, he was appointed to an additional office as preacher in the parish church. The copperplate engraving, dating from 1520, is the oldest surviving portrait of Luther. In translation the caption reads: "Luther himself immortalized the products of his mind, while Lucas's (Cranach's) depiction will fade."

■ *Fig. 18   Luther as Monk, Lucas Cranach the Elder, copperplate engraving, 1520*

Today only a part survives of the wooden *pulpit of the City Church (Fig. 19)* from which Luther began preaching against indulgences in the spring of 1517. Referring to the writs of indulgence they had bought, his parishioners insisted on absolution in confession and believed that contrition and satisfaction were no longer necessary. The indulgence controversy, hence, was sparked off by Luther's contact with the common people and by the pulpit from which he preached a large part of the around two thousand sermons that have come down to us.

On October 31, 1517, Luther wrote to his superior in the church hierarchy, Archbishop Albrecht of Magdeburg. Deeply moved by pastoral care, he pointed out the dangers that the current traffic in indulgences held for the parish. Enclosed in his letter was a manuscript with ninety-five theses he had penned as the basis for a disputation on the power and efficacy of indulgences to be held at the University of Wittenberg. The archbishop made no reply, but, suspecting heresy, forwarded the documents to Rome.

■ *Fig. 19   Martin Luther's pulpit, limewood and oak, carpentered, carved, painted, second half of the fifteenth century, on loan from the Protestant parish of Wittenberg City Church*

The planned disputation never took place. In November Luther sent the theses to scholarly friends who took them to be printed in Leipzig, Nuremberg, and Basle. The *quarto printed in Basle (Fig. 20)* on display here is one of the few surviving copies. Basically the theses discussed abuses of indulgence, not the practice as such, even though some formulations were scathing.

It was still some years before Rome set indulgences in church dogma, so Luther's theses were within his rights as a doctor of the Holy Scriptures to discuss open questions of faith. His adversaries, however, detected severe criticism of the pope in his theses, and that was considered heretical.

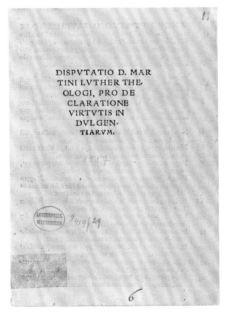

■ *Fig. 20*
Martin Luther, The Ninety-five Theses (Basle: Adam Petri, 1517)

Luther's public breakthrough only came in spring 1518 with the publication of his *Sermon on Indulgence and Grace (Ein Sermon von Ablass und Gnade)*, which was probably written at an earlier date. On eight pages Luther summarized his arguments in German. Within two years it had been reprinted twenty-two times, in Wittenberg, Augsburg, Leipzig, Nuremberg, and Basle. At the same time two Low German versions were published, as well as translations into Dutch, Danish, and Czech, while translation back into Latin finally gave the slim volume an international audience.

Suddenly Luther was a figure well-known far beyond the bounds of Wittenberg and electoral Saxony. The reasons are to be found both in the subject matter and the form of his work. Indulgences were of profound interest to laypeople, and the pamphlet's clear structure with a numbered list of arguments and plain language made it singularly apt for reading aloud. This last point was extremely important for the spread of the theses, because no more than around 10 percent of the population were literate. It was no coincidence that Luther had called his pamphlet a "sermon," even though it was not a sermon in the strict sense. The title refers to the origins of its ideas in sermons, and reflects Luther's ability to give the written word a vibrant oral quality.

The Refectory

The refectory is not part of the biographical tour, but it is one of the most impressive rooms in the house. We do not know what it looked like in Luther's time. The year inscribed in the keystone of the vault is 1565, so we may assume that the vault was constructed when the Luther House was converted for use by the university. The westernmost bay may also have been added at a later date. However, there is good reason to suppose that Luther's family and friends gathered here for their meals.

In addition to children and family, the students living in the house, servants, and friends from Wittenberg or further afield would assemble for the two main meals served every day.

Today the room is dominated by the large *panel representing the Ten Commandments* (▶ *Plate 2, pp. 35–36*). Lucas Cranach and his workshop painted the panel for the Wittenberg town council in 1516. Originally intended for the council room in the Town Hall, the panel would keep the magistrate's mind on the divine law when administering justice. The painting's representations of the individual commandments give a wealth of detail of everyday life in the early sixteenth century. The semicircle arching across the images stands for the rainbow that symbolizes the First Covenant between God and humankind as related in the story of Noah.

The way it is depicted here is unique. Both the rainbow's ends stand on the arms of electoral Saxony, showing that even before the Reformation, worldly authority was considered a good gift of God.

The individual images vividly illustrate breaches of the commandments. What is striking is the presence of angels and demons that determine human fate. A nobleman, easily identifiable by his dress and sword, is depicted repeatedly as spurning the divine commandments. The painting had, after all, been commissioned by the civil authorities, and in the early sixteenth century the relationship between the nobility and the rising cities was often strained. In Saxony, however, the elector's decisions usually favored the cities.

The two statues on the western wall of the refectory show *Moses* and *John the Baptist*. The sculptures formed part of a pulpit altar that was erected in the Castle Church after 1760 and demolished when the Castle Church was renovated in 1892.

The refectory today is a venue for lectures and concerts.

■ *Plate 2   Ten Commandments panel, Lucas Cranach the Elder (workshop), oil on wood, 1516, on loan from the City of Wittenberg*

"The time to keep silence has passed and the time to speak is come."

Luther in *An Open Letter to the Christian Nobility*, 1520

The Audition in Augsburg and the Leipzig Disputation, 1518–19

After some hesitation, Luther's colleagues at Wittenberg agreed with his criticism of indulgences. Luther's mentor in his doctoral studies, *Andreas Bodenstein Karlstadt (Fig. 21)*, was skeptical at first, but then defended Luther with such vehemence that Johann Eck, a theologian based in Ingolstadt and active proponent of the old order, challenged him first.

■ *Fig. 21*
Andreas Bodenstein Karlstadt, etching, sixteenth century

Meanwhile, formal heresy proceedings had been initiated in Rome. As Elector Frederick the Wise had no wish to jeopardize the career of his best-known professor in Wittenberg, he sought to settle the matter peaceably. He suggested a compromise. Luther was not to be summoned to Rome, but attend a "fatherly hearing" with a papal legate. In the summer of 1518 Luther therefore went to Augsburg to meet *Cardinal Cajetan (Fig. 22 ▶)*, one of the most renowned theologians of his time. However, in their debate Luther rejected all arguments based not on the Holy Scriptures but on church tradition, so that in the end he had to flee the city. The first attempt at mediation had failed. Luther felt he was right

■ *Fig. 22 Luther before Cajetan, colored woodcut, 1557*

to such an extent that very soon he had a transcript of the audience with the cardinal legate printed under the title *The Deeds of the Brother M. Luther* (*Acta Fratris M. Lutheri*). This, of course, only exacerbated the conflict.

In the meantime, Johann Eck had also challenged Luther, and the news had come to the ears of the *Saxon Duke George (Fig. 23).*

■ *Fig. 23 Duke George of Saxony, Lucas Cranach the Younger, woodcut, c. 1562*

George reigned in East Saxony. Although originally open-minded about the need for reforms in the church, he would never break with Rome, for he was not only the first cousin of the Saxon elector but also the grandson of the Bohemian king, George Podiebrad, who had been anathematized and died an excommunicated heretic. Much against the grain of the University of Leipzig, he decided to have the argument settled in a *public disputation* there *(Fig. 24)*. The clash between Luther and Johann Eck caused a sensation in academic circles.

■ *Fig. 24   The Leipzig Disputation, colored woodcut, 1557*

Public opinion turned in favor of the Wittenberg scholars, as is evident from this sympathetic portrayal of Luther in Leipzig:

"Martinus is of medium height. He has a lean frame, equally worn out by cares and studies, so that if you look closely, you can count nearly all the bones in his body. He is still of fresh and youthful age, and his voice is sharp and distinct. In company he is merry and full of wit, his untroubled face always shining blithely and cheerfully, no matter how ferocious the threats of his enemies." People thronged to listen when Luther was allowed preach in Leipzig on June 19, 1519. The sermon was soon printed in the city. Its *title page* shows the oldest surviving depiction of Luther, although it is not a portrait.

The original purpose of the disputation, to discuss indulgences, hardly played a role in the debate. Eck's intention was to unmask Luther as a heretic, and he turned the argument to the role and authority of the pope. Eck skillfully maneuvered Luther into a position where he questioned the divine appointment of the pope and asserted that heretics like John Huss (Jan Hus) were actually good Christians. The Bohemian reformer John Huss had been burned at the stake at the Council of Constance in 1415 because he had called for the church to return to its early Christian roots. Luther had aligned himself with a condemned heretic, and Eck could justifiably feel that he had publicly exposed Luther.

■ *Fig. 25 Hourglass, beech and oak, seventeenth century, on loan from the City of Wittenberg*

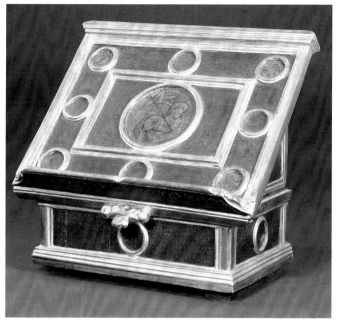

■ *Fig. 26   Lectern, wood, painted on chalk, with embossed rhombic pattern, gold leaf, seventeenth century, on loan from the Protestant parish of Wittenberg City Church*

Although the *pulpit hourglass (Fig. 25)* and the *lectern (Fig. 26)* on display here hail from a later period, they do illustrate the setting of the disputation. The lecterns of the two disputants faced each other, and each speaker was allotted a fixed amount of time to develop his arguments. The transcripts of the disputation were published in print. The University of Leipzig was unable to decide on the outcome of the debate, although the universities of Cologne and Leuven condemned Luther. Public opinion, in contrast, considered Eck the loser.

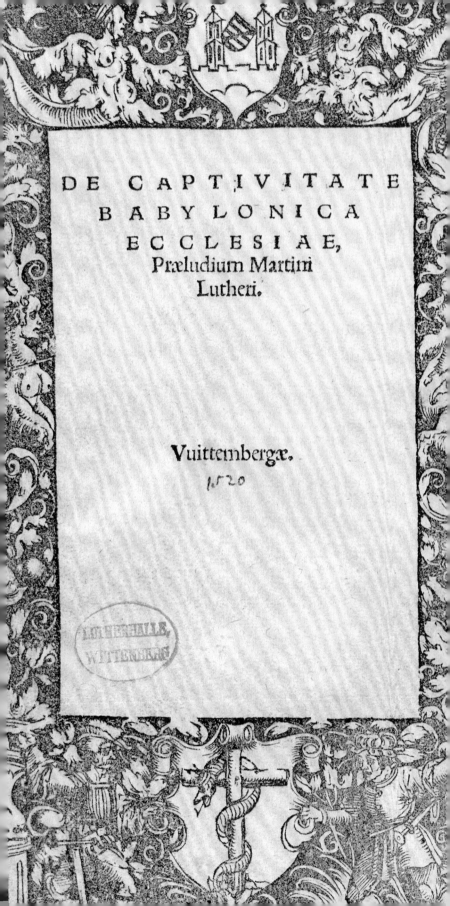

DE CAPTIVITATE
BABYLONICA
ECCLESIAE,
Præludium Martini
Lutheri.

Vuittembergæ.

1520

Key Reformatory Writings and the Burning of Church Law, 1520

The approval of his friends and the criticism of his opponents seemed to positively inspire Luther. Within a short period of time, he published a series of tracts that can be seen as the basis of his reformatory program.

He began with a treatise on ethics entitled *On Good Works (Von den guten Werken)*. This combined an interpretation of the Ten Commandments with a discussion of which good works were commendable from a biblical point of view. The distinction between faith and works is a constant feature in Luther's theology. By postulating faith as the basis of every Christian's life, he relativized the value of a life focussed primarily on religious acts.

Luther then wrote a reform program covering religious and practical life entitled *An Open Letter to the Christian Nobility of the German Nation Concerning the Reform of the Christian Estate (An den christlichen Adel deutscher Nation von des christlichen Standes Besserung)*, which questioned the previous separation of ecclesiastical and secular estates. One implication of this was that the church needed no worldly goods and had no claim to its own law. For the political authorities of the time, this held the attractive prospect of a secularization of church property.

The third pamphlet appeared in Latin with the translated title *A Prelude on the Babylonian Captivity of the Church (De captivitate babylonica ecclesiae. Praeludium, Fig. 27)*. This document represents a general offensive against the traditional church, as it criticizes the seven traditional sacraments and accepts only two as biblically justified, namely baptism and holy communion. In this way, Luther deprived the Roman Church of its popular roots, since confirmation and last rites played a large part in popular religious beliefs. His denial of marriage as a sacrament was also to have far-reaching consequences.

The fourth and probably most popular of Luther's pamphlets was entitled *On Christian Liberty (Von der Freiheit eines Christenmenschen)*. It appeared in Novem-

■ *Fig. 27   Martin Luther, The Babylonian Captivity of the Church (Wittenberg: Melchior Lotter the Younger, 1520)*

■ *Fig. 28   Pope Leo X, Papal Bull Against Luther and his Followers (Rome: Jacobus Mazochius, 1520)*

ber 1520 and outlined the new ideal of religious piety: Although the Christian lives in the world, in his faith he knows he is in God's hand alone. All four documents were reprinted several times up to 1525.

On June 15, 1520, the *Bull threatening Excommunication (Fig. 28)* was issued in Rome, giving Luther sixty days to recant his heresy. If he refused, he would be excommunicated and turned over to civil justice. Memories of the fate of John Huss were still very much alive in Saxony. The Bull also called for Luther's writings to be burned.

In Germany, the document was distributed in written form by Johann Eck and his helpers, although no one could be found for this task in the Electorate of Saxony. Luther obviously felt so confident that he asked his friend George Spalatin to print *copies of the Bull in German* in Leipzig.

After his books were publicly burned in Cologne, as shown in *a woodcut from 1524*, Luther felt emboldened

■ *Fig. 29   Luther Burns the Papal Bull, colored woodcut, 1557*

to a further act of resistance. On December 10, 1520, watched by large numbers of students, he burned works of church law and works by his opponents outside the Elster Gate. The last document he consigned to the flames was a copy of the Bull of Excommunication. An *early image of this scene (Fig. 29)* dates from 1557. As these acts suggest, Luther was convinced he had at least the same right to exclude the pope from the church as the latter had to exclude him. He supplied a public explanation for this in a tract entitled *Why the Books of the Pope and his Followers are Burned by Dr. M. Luther (Warum des Papstes und seiner Jünger Bücher von Dr. M. Luther verbrannt sind)*. Luther viewed the pope as the Antichrist prophesied in the Bible who at the end of time would take over power in the church and persecute the true believers.

Evidence of this belief is supplied by Lucas Cranach in his *Passion of Christ and Antichrist (Passional Christi und Antichristi) of 1521 (Fig. 30)*. In thirteen pairs of wood-

■ *Fig. 30   The Ascension of Christ–the Descent of the Pope into Hell, from Lucas Cranach the Elder (workshop), Passion of Christ and Antichrist (Wittenberg: Johann Rhau-Grunenberg, 1521)*

cuts, the life of Christ as described in the gospels is contrasted with the life of the Renaissance popes. Christ enters Jerusalem as the Prince of Peace, while the pope (clearly a reference to Julius II) is one of the greatest military commanders of his time. Christ drives the money changers out of the temple, while the pope is involved in banking (a reference to Leo X whose family, the Medici, achieved power and prestige through financial dealings). Logically enough, then, the series concludes by juxtaposing the Ascension of Christ with the pope's descent into hell.

This mode of representation also prefigures later problems. Luther had always emphasized that the papacy should be overthrown by spiritual means only, using the word of God. But this is not born out at all clearly in the polemic series of images. On the contrary, viewers who could not read, making them unable to follow Luther's distinctions, must have seen the sequence as a call to take their fate into their own hands. And although Luther's attacks were always aimed solely at the ecclesiastical authorities, this aspect is insufficiently clear in the woodcuts and could easily be missed by a cursory viewer. This marked the beginning of a fundamental misunderstanding that culminated in the Peasants' Revolt, where the rebels cited Luther's teachings as their authority.

"And since my conscience is captive to the Word of God, I neither can nor will recant anything, for to go against one's conscience is neither right nor safe. So help me, God. Amen."

Luther on April 18, 1521, before the Diet of Worms

Worms — Before Emperor and Empire, 1521

According to the custom of the time, excommunication was followed by an imperial ban declaring the person in question an outlaw, meaning that anyone was allowed to kill him without punishment. In addition, his friends were forbidden to help him.

In the case of Luther, Elector Frederick the Wise once again successfully intervened, this time with *Emperor Charles V (Fig. 31)*. As king of Spain and grandson to the

■ *Fig. 31 Emperor Charles V, copy by Minna Pfüller after Christoph Amberger, oil on canvas, second half of the 19th century*

Habsburg emperor, Maximilian I, Charles had acceded to the throne in 1519 after difficult negotiations. In the dispute with his rivals Francis I of France and Henry VIII of England, he was forced to make considerable concessions to the powerful electors of Germany. These included the assurance that no subject of the empire would be judged by a foreign court.

It was this assurance to which the elector of Saxony appealed. As Archmarshal of the Empire, his wishes had a special weight even among the electors. As a result, Frederick was able to secure a hearing for his Wittenberg professor at the Diet of Worms, as well as an assurance of safe passage for his journey there and back.

■ *Fig. 32 Martin Luther, Lucas Cranach the Elder, oil on wood, c. 1520, on loan from the State of Saxony-Anhalt / East German Saving Bank Foundation in the State of Saxony-Anhalt, and the Wittenberg Saving Bank*

On April 17, 1521, *Martin Luther stood before the assembled estates of the Empire (Fig. 32 and detail on the cover).* This portrait shows him in a monk's habit with a doctor's cap and no beard. It is a rarity, as only two

■ *Fig. 33 Habit allegedly worn by Luther, woolen fabric, sixteenth century*

other pictures of this type are known.

The *habit (Fig. 33)* is said to have been Luther's own. It certainly dates from the early sixteenth century and belonged to the Augustinian order. Whether Luther himself wore it can not be established for sure.

Although he was only twenty-one years old, Charles V was the most powerful man of his time. His was an empire on which the sun literally never set, including colonies in Central and South America. The *folding chair (Fig. 34 ►)* and the *coconut cup (Fig. 35 ►)* are reminders of this power.

According to the appointed procedure, the official of the Archbishop of Trier, Johann von der Ecken (not to be mistaken with Luther's old rival Johann Eck), read out the titles from a pile of Luther's works. Luther admitted that he was their author. When asked to recant his writings, he surprised all present by requesting a day's time to decide. After some hesitation, his request was granted. The next day, he declared in a quiet voice, "Since my con-

■ *Fig. 34 Folding chair, northern foothills of the Alps or Tyrol, beech, early sixteenth century*

■ *Fig. 35 Coconut goblet, Christoff Ritterle, Nuremberg, gilt silver, c. 1560*

science is captive to the Word of God, I neither can nor will recant anything, for to go against one's conscience is neither right nor safe. So help me, God. Amen." The famous words "Here I stand. I cannot do otherwise" were added to the story at a later date. These words can be seen on a *depiction of the scene dating from 1557 (Fig. 36).*

■ *Fig. 36   Luther at the Imperial Diet in Worms, colored woodcut, 1557*

His refusal to recant and his reference to his own conscience against all churchly and worldly authority were to change the course of world history. Suprisingly the young emperor was particularly aware of this. To the surprise of his councilors, he answered Luther with a short address in Latin that he had written himself, declaring his steadfast loyalty to the Old Church. Later, he explained to his entourage: "The dirty monk shall not make a heretic of me." But Charles kept his promise and allowed Luther to leave Worms unharmed.

Had he done otherwise, there would surely have been a riot. Public opinion in Worms was unreservedly on Luther's side, as noted by the Papal nuncio Hieronymus Aleander. It was also shown by an unprecedented flood of *pamphlets* reporting and commenting on Luther's appearance in Worms, and comparing him to St. Paul, Daniel, and a German Hercules. He was, without a doubt, at the absolute peak of his popularity.

It is therefore no surprise that the official edict against Luther was not issued until after the end of the Diet, when the elector of Saxony had already departed. In view of the actual climate of opinion in the Empire, the edict represented wishes more than orders. Returning from Worms, Luther himself wrote a long *letter to the emperor (Fig. 37)*, stating once again why he was unable to recant on his writings. Although the letter explicitly thanks the emperor for the safe passage granted to him, the elector's secretary George Spalatin could find no one willing to hand it over to its addressee. In spite of this, a printed version soon appeared. In 1911, the manuscript was bought at an auction in Leipzig by the American multimillionaire Pierpoint Morgan and offered to Kaiser Wilhelm II. To raise the value of his gift, Morgan sent two agents who were unaware of each other to bid against one another, driving the price up to 102,000 gold marks, a huge sum at the time. In return, he received the Order of the Red Eagle from the German Kaiser, and the letter was donated to the Lutherhalle in Wittenberg.

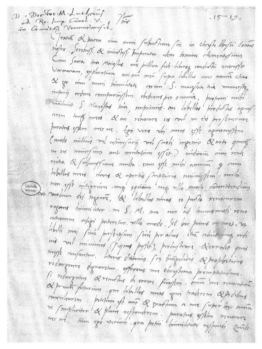

■ *Fig. 37   Martin Luther, letter to Emperor Charles V,
Friedberg, April 28, 1521*

Luther at Wartburg Castle, 1521–22

Although the elector of Saxony was neither willing nor able to publicly resist an edict from the emperor, the fate of his professor was a matter of great personal importance to him. The solution was for Luther to spend a lengthy period at Wartburg Castle. It is most probable that Frederick the Wise knew no details, so that he could inform the public with a clear conscience that he did not know of Luther's whereabouts.

On May 4, 1521, Luther was "kidnapped" by armed men near Altenstein in Thuringia and taken to Wartburg Castle. In the sixteenth century, this fortress was of no great importance. There was only a small garrison stationed there, with whom the secret of the castle's new inhabitant was safe. Luther let his hair and beard grow and wore the clothes of a knight. The monk became "Junker Jörg" (Knight George), as painted by Cranach in the late fall of 1521. This picture was used by Heinrich Göding the Elder as the basis for an *engraving in 1598 (Fig. 38).*

■ *Fig. 38   Luther as Knight George before Worms, Heinrich Göding the Elder, etching, 1598*

Das Newe Testament Deutzsch

Wittemberg.

Many of Luther's contemporaries, including Albrecht Dürer, believed he had been secretly murdered. Luther himself was now comparing himself with the Apostle John, who lived in exile on the island of Patmos. He also wrote a series of important works, including a *statement on monastic vows* and a detailed explanation of the sermons for the beginning of the church year, the *Advent Postil (Adventpostille).* Although Luther complained in his letters about the unfamiliar lifestyle, and especially about the food, this did not prevent him from working intensively.

Luther's most important work at Wartburg Castle was his translation of the *New Testament* into German. Writing from Wittenberg, Philipp Melanchthon had encouraged him to undertake this task. Although German translations of the Bible had been in print since the late fifteenth century, they were based on the Latin text of the Vulgate. Luther used the Greek text first published in 1516 by Erasmus of Rotterdam (the "Prince of Humanists") together with the Latin text. He completed a rough version of the translation in just twelve weeks. In March 1522, Luther took the work with him to Wittenberg, where he reworked it for printing with Melanchthon, whose knowledge of Greek was superior to his own. From May through September, the printer Melchior Lotter worked in the house of Lucas Cranach on the unusually large edition of three thousand copies *(Fig. 39)*. This edition sold out so fast that a further fifteen hundred copies had to be printed in December. Lucas Cranach decorated the 444-page folio with twenty-one woodcuts of the Apocalypse, raising the price to 2.5 florins. But this high price did not affect sales: by 1524, the translation of the New Testament had been through sixty-six printings in Germany.

Luther's greatest literary success is commemorated in an *engraving by Wolfgang Stuber from around 1580 depicting Luther as Saint Jerome (Fig. 40 ▶)*. In a mirrored version of the famous image by Albrecht Dürer, it is now Luther in his cell who creates an epoch-making work, like St. Jerome did before him with the Vulgate.

■ *Fig. 39   Martin Luther, The German New Testament (September Testament) (Wittenberg: Melchior Lotter the Younger, 1522)*

PESTIS * ERAM * VIVVS
MORIENS * TVA * MORS * ERO * PAPA

"Should the word of God only be subjected to endless discussion and never put into action?"
Luther from the Wartburg to Spalatin, mid-December 1521

The Wittenberg Movement and Luther's Return, 1522

During Luther's absence, his supporters in Wittenberg, especially Andreas Karlstadt, Philipp Melanchthon, and the Augustinian monk Gabriel Zwilling, began carrying out concrete reforms. Under the influence of Luther's writings, the first priests began to marry and monks left their monasteries, so that in 1523 both the Gray Cloister of the Franciscans and the Black Cloister of the Augustinians stood empty. Monastic vows and the marriage of priests were discussed by ordinary people. In 1522, Johann Eberlin published a pamphlet entitled *How it Be Dangerous if a Priest Has No Wife* (*Wie gar gefährlich sei, so ein Priester kein Eheweib hat*, Fig. 41). A woodcut on the title page shows a marriage between a monk and a nun.

At Christmas 1521, Karlstadt celebrated the first evangelical communion where the laity were offered the chalice. Almost the entire population of Wittenberg attended the City Church. The services now also regularly included sermons.

■ *Fig. 41   Johann Eberlin, How it Be Dangerous if a Priest Has No Wife (Augsburg: Melchior Ramminger, 1522)*

■ *Fig. 40   Luther as St. Jerome, Wolfgang Stuber, copperplate engraving, c. 1580*

The city was seen by its inhabitants not only as a place, but also as an organism. The forms of religious life and the structure of public life had consequences for the fate of the community. These ideas survived into the post-Reformation period, as documented by the inscription on a *view of Wittenberg around 1558 (Fig. 42)*:

"Wittenberg, the glorious city of God, seat and fortress of the true doctrine that rules the globe, the capital city of the Electorate of Saxony, the most famous of Europe's universities, and by far the holiest place of the last millennium."

■ *Fig. 42   View of Wittenberg, Cranach workshop, colored wood-cut, c. 1558*

Under pressure from the population, the city of Wittenberg gave itself a *new civic code* without heeding the rights of the elector. The new code focused primarily on reforming life within the community: beggars from elsewhere were to be expelled from the city; the municipal brothel was closed; a *common chest was set up to help the city's poor and to ensure orderly administration of church revenues (Fig. 43)*.

Even after the elector revoked the code, this institution remained. Luther was explicitly in favor of it and in 1523 he wrote a separate *set of regulations* for the common chest in the city of Leisnig. Church revenues, which were now all collected in a single fund, were administered on an equal basis by the city council, the parish, and the clergy. They were used to pay the pastors and for the up-

■ *Fig. 43   Common chest of the city of Wittenberg, iron chest with three separate locks, c. 1520, on loan from the City of Wittenberg*

keep of the church buildings, but also for helping the poor and nursing the sick. Craftsmen were granted low-interest loans according to the principle of "helping people help themselves." Support was also provided to help poor parents send their children to school. Social neediness was subject to rigorous checks by the treasurer according to the principle: "He who does not work, neither shall he eat." In the Old Church, poverty was seen as an opportunity for good works by giving alms. Beggars were literally organized in guilds. The end of the idea that alms for the poor were a way of earning merit brought a more rational approach to dealing with poverty. A woodcut entitled *An Admonition for the Young (Fig. 44 ▶)* portrays poverty less as fate than as a consequence of a bad life.

A written record was kept of the fund's transactions. A *receipt from 1531* documents revenues. The records surviving at Wittenberg City Church show that the system functioned satisfactorily, at least in the sixteenth century.

More controversial was the question of reforming the order of service. With reference to the biblical ban on idolatry, radical groups began campaigning for the removal of icons from churches. Karlstadt supported this movement with his tract *On the Removal of Images (Von Abtu-*

■ *Fig. 44 An Admonition for the Young, woodcut, first half of the sixteenth century, excerpt*

ung der Bilder). The *double pietà* shown here (Fig. 45) is a reminder of the problem. According to Christoph Scheurl, a similar sculpture once stood in the Castle Church but was destroyed by iconoclasts.

Luther himself thought that worshipping saints broke the first commandment. He rejected the worship of statues and images. Nonetheless, he showed deep reverence for Mary throughout his life. In Luther's view, the form of church services and the appearance of the church itself was a matter for the congregation to decide, as he explained in his 1523 tract *On the Right and Power of a Christian Congregation or Parish to Judge all Doctrine and to Appoint and Dismiss Teachers, for Reasons Based on Holy Scripture* (*Dass eine christliche Versammlung oder Gemeinde Recht und Macht habe, alle Lehre zu urteilen und Lehrer zu berufen, ein- und abzusetzen, Grund und Ursache aus der Schrift*).

What Luther found far more problematic was the danger to evangelical freedoms. He returned to Wittenberg in March 1522 against the will of the elector. In his so-called *Invocavit sermons*, he expressed his opposition to the new legislative character of the reforms.

Under Luther's influence, the pace of the reforms slowed down. Step-by-step changes met with the approval of the large majority of the population. The only resistance came from the Collegiate Chapter of All Saints and lasted until 1525.

■ *Fig. 45 Double pietà, wood, carved, sixteenth century*

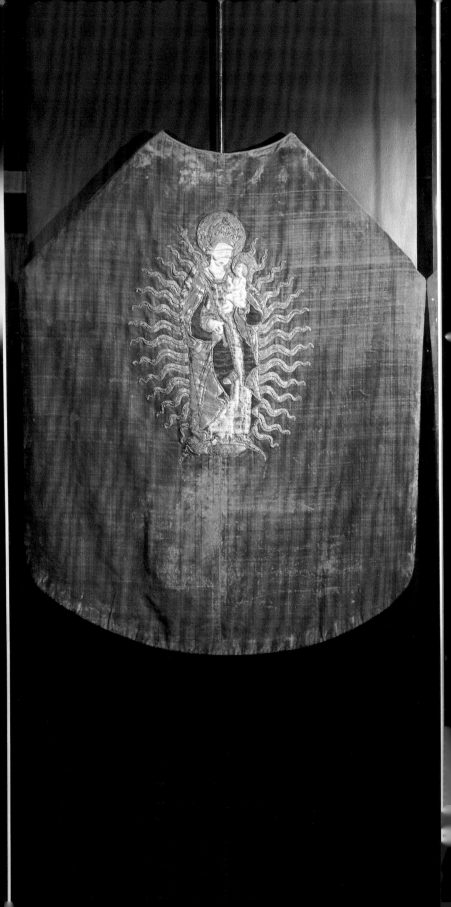

"Let spirits clash . . . But let fists be silent!"

Luther, 1524

Reforms in the Parish, 1523–25

The traditional church service, centered around the Mass, made a strict distinction between clergy and laity. With his surplice and richly decorated *chasuble (Fig. 46)*, the priest was set apart from the simple believers, who remained passive spectators. The liturgy for Holy Communion, laid down in a sumptuously *decorated missal*, was held in Latin, and as such the congregation did not understand it. At the Eucharist, they were only given the bread, as it was feared that the wine, the true blood of Christ, could be spilled.

As a first step, Luther introduced sermons as part of every church service, regularly taking to the pulpit himself. In this way, interpretation of the word of God took an equal place beside the sacrament. At the weekly services, the catechism was explained to educate believers. In his treatise *On the Order of Service in the Parish (Von Ordnung des Gottesdiensts in der Gemeinde)*, Luther explained that where there was any doubt, anything that might be detrimental to propagating the Word of God should be avoided. It was therefore only logical that he opposed masses financed by wealthy parishioners, especially when they were held with no participation from the congregation as "silent Mass." The abolition of silent Mass made a large portion of the church's staff redundant.

Luther also abolished obligatory confession, although until his death he himself confessed regularly to Johann Bugenhagen. Later, Luther replaced confession with an admonition to communicants before Holy Communion, to ensure that the congregation was aware of its importance.

Holy Communion now offered the chalice to the laity. A *woodcut from around 1550 (Fig. 49 ▶)* shows Luther together with John Huss at Communion. In spite of its historical inaccuracy, this image is a reminder that the

■ *Fig. 46 Chasuble with image of the Virgin Mary, silk velvet, embroidered, fifteenth or sixteenth century, on loan from the Protestant parish of Zwochau*

■ Fig. 47 Communion cup, Martin Baumgärtner, gilt silver,
sixteenth century/1636

■ Fig. 48 Corn Extortion, Daniel Hopfer, copperplate engraving, 1534

Hussites in the fifteenth century had already campaigned for the laity to receive the chalice. This change meant that larger *chalices had to be made (Fig. 47)*, often keeping the same stem and simply enlarging the upper part.

With the introduction of evangelical hymns, Luther gave the laity a voice within the act of worship. Although he in no way favored abolishing the existing professional choirs, he considered it of major importance to give the congregation an active role. In 1524, the first *Protestant hymnbook* appeared in Wittenberg. In a preface, Luther praised the arts. Evangelical hymns certainly played an outstanding part in the spread and triumph of the Reformation. From 1523, Luther began composing such hymns, and in some cases also set them to music himself.

These liturgical reforms were accompanied by a program of social and school reform. Luther's programmatic tract *On Commerce and Usury (Von Kaufhandlung und Wucher)* aimed to reform business customs. His main emphasis was on the lower strata of society and he considered it a duty of the parish to keep them supplied with grain for breadmaking. The importance of this issue is illustrated by Daniel Hopfer's engraving entitled *Corn Extortion (Fig. 48)*.

The reform of the church had direct economic consequences. Sebald Beham caricatures this in his woodcut *Members of the Roman Church Complain About Luther*: artists and craftsmen lose contracts for building and decorating churches; a peasant stands on Luther's side. Beham also created the *allegory on the luxuriant lives of monks*: a peasant, driven by hunger, forces a book down the throat of a monk held fast by greed, pride, and craving for pleasure.

Luther's school reforms were more successful than his economic reforms. His appeal *To the Councilmen of All Cities in Germany That They Establish and Maintain Christian Schools (An die Ratsherren aller Städte deutschen Landes, dass sie christliche Schulen aufrichten und halten sollen)* laid the foundations for a development that later led to an extensive system of elementary

schools in Germany. Luther's use of theological arguments was of key importance here. Since every individual was answerable for his or her own faith, everyone
(including the female section of the population, a revolutionary step) had to be able to read and write in order to
understand the Holy Scriptures him or herself. Each
parish was to be assigned a school. This also applied
to villages, where around 80 percent of the population
lived and where there had previously been no schools at
all. Peasants in particular were only likely to send their
children to school for religious reasons at best. In economic terms, it made more sense for them to put their
offspring to work in the fields at as early an age as possible.

The school reform was followed by the reform of the
university in Wittenberg, which is associated above all
with the name of Philipp Melanchthon. The courses at the
Faculty of Arts in particular underwent major changes to
meet new requirements: instead of priests ordained by
the church, there was now demand for pastors with a
university education.

■ *Fig. 49 Luther and Huss Administering the Sacrament in Both
Ways, Cranach workshop, woodcut, c. 1550*

The Peasants' Revolt and Thomas Müntzer, 1525

In the course of the Reformation, existing social conflicts were aggravated and new ones emerged. Luther's concept of Christian or evangelical liberty was increasingly interpreted in political terms, especially in southern Germany, where uprisings began in 1524. As the peasants saw it, the new doctrine made serfdom intolerable. Luther himself dealt with the issue in 1523 in a tract entitled *Worldly Authority and the Limits to Obedience (Von weltlicher Obrigkeit, wie weit man ihr Gehorsam schuldig sei)*. Interpreting Romans, chapter 13, he qualified worldly authority in principle as a gift of God, but forbade it to reign over souls. Reforms were to be carried out by the word of God alone, without any violence.

Thomas Müntzer (Fig. 50), first a student in Leipzig and Wittenberg and later a parish priest in Allstedt, came to a different conclusion.

■ *Fig. 50   Thomas Müntzer, Christoffel van Sichem, etching, 1608*

In his view, the spirit of God should find its place in the hearts of the chosen ones, who were to make this possible by purging themselves of the desire for wealth, power, and glory, before going on to rigorously fight the godless. Müntzer saw the outbreak of the Peasants' Revolt as the work of God, although he thought that *The Fundamental and Just Demands of the Peasantry* (*Die gründlichen und rechten Hauptartikel aller Bauernschaft*), the written program of the south German peasants, did not go far enough. Before the uprising, Luther had read and welcomed this treatise, also known as the Twelve Articles.

In the spring of 1525, the revolt spread to Thuringia. In his appeal entitled *Admonition to Peace, a Reply to the Twelve Articles of the Peasants in Swabia* (*Ermahnung zum Frieden auf die zwölf Artikel der Bauernschaft in Schwaben*), Luther urged both sides to conciliation. But by the time the appeal appeared, blood had already been shed. Luther then spoke out again in *Against the Murderous and Thieving Hordes of Peasants* (*Wider die räuberischen und mörderischen Rotten der anderen Bauern*), as he considered any uprising of subjects against their authorities to be biblically unacceptable. Once again, his words came too late. By the time they were published, the Peasants' Revolt had already been crushed in the bloodbath of Frankenhausen.

■ *Fig. 51*   *Halberds and spears, sixteenth century, cuirass and closed helmet, iron, etched, c. 1520, on loan from the City of Eisleben*

■ *Fig. 52   Gun barrel, cast iron, sixteenth century, on loan from the City of Eisleben*

The rebels were powerless against the elector's lansquenets who were *much better armed (Figs. 51, 52)*. Thomas Müntzer, who accompanied the peasants as a preacher, was captured and executed. In the public view, Luther's writings were seen as justifying the princes' cruelty against the defeated peasants.

Without a doubt, the Peasants' Revolt dealt a blow to Luther's popularity. He, on the other hand, learned from these events always to side with the authorities in case of doubt, so as to prevent a repeat of the conflict. At the height of the uprising, Elector Frederick the Wise died. He was succeeded by his *brother John (Fig. 54 ▶)*, a resolute advocate of Luther's positions. In 1532, he was succeeded by his son *John Frederick the Magnanimous (Fig. 55 ▶)*. Luther saw the *Wittenberg executioner's sword (Fig. 53)* as a symbol of worldly authority. In his view, its task was to protect the good and punish the evil.

■ *Fig. 53   Sword, wrought iron and steel, turned wood, sixteenth century*

■ *Fig. 54* *John the Steadfast, Prince Elector of Saxony, Lucas Cranach the Elder (workshop), oil on wood, sixteenth century, excerpt*

■ *Fig. 55* *John Frederick the Magnanimous, Prince Elector of Saxony, monogram master IS (Cranach workshop), oil on wood, sixteenth century, excerpt*

■ *Plate 3* *Large Lecture Hall with disputation lectern by Jacob Johann Marchand, wood, carved and painted, after 1685*

Large Lecture Hall

Although this room is not part of the biographical tour, its function and decoration are a reminder of Luther's activity as a professor in Wittenberg. It is most likely that Luther gave lectures at the Black Cloister until around 1520. In the nineteenth century, Friedrich August Stüler converted the room into a memorial hall. The Baroque *university lectern with paintings by Jacob Johann Marchand* (◄ *Plate 3, p. 71–72*) dates from around 1687. The pictures of *the four electors (Fig. 56)* are older, although it cannot be said with certainty whether they were created specially for this hall. The same applies to the series of *portraits of professors (Fig. 57 ►)* that have been on display here since 1983. The three *sixteenth-century silken flags* are unique and most valuable. The first was used by the entire university, the second by the Faculty of Arts. The *third (Fig. 58 ►)* belonged to the Association of Hungarian Students, the largest association of non-German students at Wittenberg University.

■ *Fig. 56   Frederick III the Wise, Prince Elector of Saxony, Lucas Cranach the Younger, oil on canvas, c. 1570, on loan from the Wittenberg Preachers Seminary, excerpt*

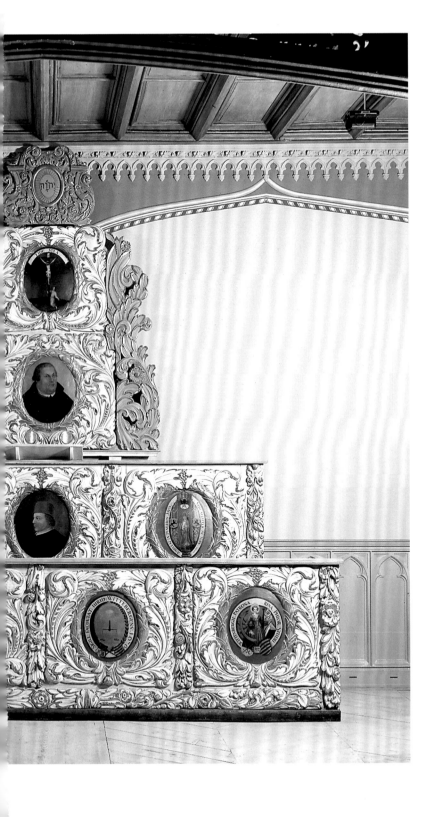

■ *Fig. 57   Martin Pollich von Mellerstadt (?-1513), physician, first rector of the university, oil on limewood, c. 1608, on loan from the Wittenberg Preachers Seminary, excerpt*

■ *Fig. 58   Flag of the Hungarian students' association, sixteenth century, on loan from the Wittenberg Preachers Seminary*

"All that makes a man needs to have a woman and all that makes a woman also needs to have a man."

Luther, 1522, On Married Life

Marriage and Family, 1525–46

This room, together with the next two, formed the heart of the private quarters after Luther and his family settled in the former monastery. This room was probably a bedroom. The two *pine closets* date from Luther's time.

■ *Fig. 59   Martin Luther, On Married Life (Augsburg: Heinrich Steiner, 1523)*

Although Luther started calling for the right of marriage for priests and monks in 1521, he hesitated to heed his own advice, even though his sermon *On Married Life (Vom ehelichen Leben, Fig. 59)* points out the necessity of marriage. Luther's praise of matrimony as the divine order put a radical end to a long ecclesiastical tradition of sexual abstinence.

At Easter 1523 nine nuns fled from the convent of Nimbschen near Grimma and came to Wittenberg asking for assistance. Luther managed to find husbands for most of them, thus saving them from destitution. In his *Why Nuns Should Leave Convents as a Matter of Faith (Ursache und Antwort, dass Jungfrauen Klöster göttlich verlassen mögen)* he defends his actions and names the nuns. Among them was Katharina von Bora, who came from an old but impoverished Saxon noble family and had lived in the convent since childhood. The exhibited *rosary* is said to have belonged to her, but this cannot be established with certainty.

Luther married Katharina von Bora on June 13, 1525, completely out of the blue. Apparently he thought this step would improve relations with his father, who had disapproved of his joining a religious order. It was also the height of the Peasants' Revolt, and Luther, fearing that he might not have long to live, wanted to reinforce his teachings by putting them into practice. The deciding factor, however, may have been Katharina's insistence that if she did not marry Luther or his friend Nikolaus von Amsdorf she would prefer to remain single.

For Luther's enemies, his marriage was a scandal. Even his friends were critical, especially Philipp Melanchthon. The university, on the other hand, presented its professor with a *silver goblet* as a wedding gift.

■ *Fig. 60 Martin Luther, Lucas Cranach the Elder, oil on wood, 1525*

■ *Fig. 61 Katharina von Bora, Lucas Cranach the Elder (workshop), oil on wood, 1528, excerpt*

■ *Fig. 62 Martin Luther, Lucas Cranach the Elder (workshop), oil on wood, 1528, excerpt*

For the wedding Lucas Cranach painted a double portrait of the couple in a small round format, but only *Luther's is in the Wittenberg collections today* (◄ *Fig. 60*). It is without doubt one of the best portraits of the Reformer. After 1528 the elector commissioned Cranach to paint a series of *double portraits of the couple* (◄ *Figs. 61, 62*) in rectangular format.

These paintings were taken as gifts when visiting allied courts, and served to propagate the idea that the former monk and former nun were legally and properly married. That is why relatively many oil portraits of Luther's wife have been handed down to posterity, whereas there are no depictions of Melanchthon's or Bugenhagen's spouse. Contemporary artists such as Hans Brosamer subsequently made *woodcuts from the paintings (Fig. 63)*. There was plainly also a commercial interest in Katharina's countenance.

■ *Fig. 63 Katharina von Bora, after Hans Brosamer, woodcut, after 1530*

The couple produced six children; three boys and three girls. Four reached adulthood, which, considering that infant mortality was around 30 percent at that time, suggests that there was enough to eat in the Luther household even in these difficult early years. The death of his daughter Magdalena at the age of twelve was a blow to Luther. His lamentations for her are probably the reason why the *girl in the portrait (Fig. 64)*, a sixteenth-century copy after Cranach, was believed to be Magdalena.

■ *Fig. 64   Portrait of a girl, after Lucas Cranach the Elder, 1520, oil on wood, sixteenth century, copy*

After 1530 the family's financial circumstances improved. Luther's salary was raised several times, and the elector sent regular gifts, especially of food and textiles. Katharina took in students who paid for board and lodging, and the household accounts show that she brought in at least as much income as Luther did with his salary.

This is when the house started filling up with interesting and valuable purchases and gifts. Not one of the exhibited pieces actually comes from Luther's household, but they show the kind of possessions he owned. For example, a letter shows that the family's cash was kept in an iron *casket like the exhibited one from Nuremberg (Fig. 65)*.

■ *Fig. 65   Casket, Nuremberg, sheet iron, etched, sixteenth century*

According to his own account, Luther had to buy new kitchen utensils and crockery, because the Black Cloister's original furnishings had been looted at some point after 1521. The new acquisitions included a *mortar and pestle (Fig. 66)* for crushing spices, several ceramic and metal *pipkins*, the *rounded jar*, and the *earthenware bowl*.

The round, *hammered brass platter (Fig. 67)* was quite a luxury item. Despite its religious decoration it was not

■ *Fig. 66 Mortar and pestle, southern Europe, cast brass, first half of the sixteenth century*

used as a baptismal basin. Instead, it was used to serve the main courses at banquets. A great number of such bowls have survived, which suggests that they were widespread but seldom used.

■ *Fig. 67 Brass platter, Nuremberg, hammered, early sixteenth century*

The brass *aquamanile (Fig. 68)*, which guests at table used to pour water over their hands, and the *metal candlestick* were probably also reserved for the banquet table.

Wax candles were expensive, so pine torches were generally used for everyday purposes. They were smoky

■ *Fig. 68   Aquamanile, cast brass, sixteenth century*

and gave off little light.

The *ceramic pitcher* was one of the more luxuriously decorated household items. A *padlock* and a *wooden lantern* of the type shown here may well have also been found in Luther's household.

It is known that Luther owned a *weapon* similar to the one on display. In the sixteenth century citizens were not permitted to bear arms in public, but they were allowed, indeed required to keep a long knife for self-defense in the home. It is also known that Luther possessed a number of timepieces. He was given one by an admirer in 1527, and another in 1529. We do not, however, know whether these were *table clocks like the one shown here (Fig. 69)* or pocket watches (which had just been invented).

By the end of his life Luther was one of Wittenberg's wealthiest citizens, thanks to the efforts of Katharina von Bora. When he drew up his will in 1542 he already estimated his fortune to amount to nine thousand florins. His

■ *Fig. 69   Clock, Germany, iron, first half of the sixteenth century*

collection of gold and silver beakers and ornaments alone was valued at one thousand florins.

The largest single item was six thousand florins for the Black Cloister, which had been made over to him in 1532, but Luther was overoptimistic in assessing the value of his real estate. When his heirs sold their family home to the elector in 1564 they had to be satisfied with less. The *deed of sale (Fig. 70)* bears the seals of Luther's sons, which, like their father's, use the rose motif.

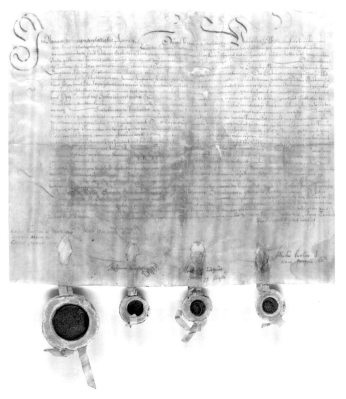

■ *Fig. 70   Deed of sale of Luther's house to the university by his sons for 3,700 florins, Wittenberg, September 27, 1564, parchment*

■ *Plate 4   Luther's living room*

Luther's living room

To this day this large paneled room conveys something of the Luther family's prosperity. Even if the painted coffered ceiling was only added after Luther's death and the tiled stove dates from 1602, the wooden paneling gives an idea of a family living in comfortable circumstances here. The lead glazed windows represented a luxury that probably did not originally extend to the whole house. In winter the small sliding openings allowed for ventilation without too much of the valuable warmth escaping. The ornamentation on the doors, with carved palmettes at the top, points to the Renaissance. It is said that Peter the Great, czar of Russia, wrote his *name* on the west door.

In the sixteenth century, even the wealthier untitled families had little in the way of furniture, so the *big table and the throne chair may well correspond to the original furnishing* (◄ *Plate 4, pp. 85–86),* although one could imagine a couple of simple chairs and maybe a chest as well. The table and the throne chair date from the sixteenth century, although they must have been restored and altered at a later date. By the seventeenth century this room had acquired the name "Museum Lutheri." The university professors met here to mark the anniversary of the Reformation and the room was shown to visiting travelers.

"Others carry my burden, their strength is my strength."
Luther, 1520

Luther's Friends

Despite working long hours alone at his desk, Martin Luther loved company. During his earlier life in the monastery, he was surrounded by his fellow monks; later, as a family man, by his children and friends. To Luther these people were the kernel of the Christian community. They prayed and sang together, and this is also where he found his retreat from struggle.

His two most important friends were Philipp Melanchthon and Johann Bugenhagen. Melanchthon, whose real name was Schwarzerd, came to Wittenberg in 1518 at Luther's initiative to occupy the new chair of Greek at the university. Despite their difference in age they developed a close working relationship, which led Melanchthon to become Luther's most important ally.

Melanchthon ignored Luther's admonitions to move to the Faculty of Theology, instead continuing to teach grammar and rhetoric to all the students, as well as reading the classical poets and philosophers. Thus Melanchthon was the real teacher of Germany, indeed of Europe.

The first of a series of *double portraits of these two reformers (Figs. 71, 72* ▶) was made in connection with the Diet of Augsburg of 1530. The elector commissioned the paintings from the workshop of Lucas Cranach to demonstrate that the theological teachings of the two men formed a unity, although in reality differences certainly existed.

Luther maintained a lifelong friendship with *Johann Bugenhagen (Fig. 73* ▶) from Pomerania. In 1523 Bugenhagen was appointed pastor of Wittenberg's City Church at Luther's insistence, against the resistance of the unreformed Collegiate Chapter of All Saints. Later he also became a professor at the university. His name is associated above all with the Reformation and renewal of the churches of northern Germany and Denmark.

■ *Fig. 71   Martin Luther, Lucas Cranach the Elder (workshop), oil on wood, 1540*

■ Fig. 73   Johannes Bugenhagen, Lucas Cranach the Elder, oil on
beech, 1537, on loan from the Wittenberg Preachers
Seminary, excerpt

■ Fig. 74   Luther's tankard, turned root wood, first half of the sixteenth century, silver mounting, 1694

■ Fig. 72   Philipp Melanchthon, Lucas Cranach the Elder (workshop), oil on wood, 1540

The friends met regularly at Luther's house to dine and discuss, probably moving to the living room after the meal. Katharina von Bora was the only woman to participate regularly.

In 1526 the students began to write down these meal-time conversations, which were published in heavily edited form after Luther's death. This "table talk" represents an important source of information on Luther's everyday life, albeit one to be treated with caution. His mealtime companions, especially the students, not only respected Luther, but revered and venerated him. They collected examples of his handwriting and even items from his household.

One such "relic" is *Luther's tankard* (◄ *Fig. 74).* In 1694 an admirer of Luther had the simple root wood vessel provided with a silver mounting inscribed with the words "THIS JAR WAS USED AT TABLE BY THE BLESSED MISTER LUTHERUS IN EISLEBEN." It is known from correspondence that Luther had wood-turning tools sent from Nuremberg in 1527, but there is no proof that he made the tankard himself.

Drinks played an important role in the table talk. Luther himself often praised the good beer brewed by his wife. Another *tankard (Fig. 75)* and a *glass* show the high quality of craftsmanship in Luther's time.

■ *Fig. 75   Stoneware tankard, Siegburg, stoneware, white, cut and molded, second half of the sixteenth century*

"Believe in Christ, and do your duty in that state of life to which God has called you."

Luther, Table Talk 1531–32

Luther's Contribution to the Reformation, 1526–46

From 1535 until shortly before his death Luther taught The First Book of Moses at the university. The first edition of the *Lectures on Genesis (Genesisvorlesung)*, his monumental late work, appeared in 1544. A *portrait from the Cranach workshop (Fig. 76)* was made at about the same time, and shows the Reformer older but still vigorous.

A similar depiction of Luther is found in the *woodcut by Jacob Lucius (Fig. 77 ►)*, which shows the baptism of Christ not in the River Jordan, but in the Elbe near Wittenberg, with the elector and his family present as witnesses.

Together with Philipp Melanchthon, Luther wrote the

■ *Fig. 76   Martin Luther, Lucas Cranach the Elder (workshop), oil on wood, c. 1541*

■ *Fig. 77* *The Baptism of Christ with Luther and the Family of the
Elector John Frederick, after Jacob Lucius, woodcut,
second half of the sixteenth century*

first Protestant church regulations in 1528, the *Instruc-
tions for the Visitors of Parish Pastors in Electoral Saxony
(Unterricht der Visitatoren an die Pfarrherren im Kurfür-
stentum Sachsen)*. In his preface Luther stressed that a
new form of church leadership had still to be found. For
that reason, he wrote, the secular rulers should take on
the supervision of the Church as "emergency bishops."

In 1529 Luther published one of his most influential
works, The *Large Catechism (Der Große Katechismus)*.
Here, in a pithy question-and-answer form, he explains
Christian basic knowledge through the Ten Commandments, the creed, and the Lord's Prayer.

In the lead-up to the Diet of Augsburg of 1530, it seemed that a reconciliation with the conservatives might be
possible. To further that end Melanchthon, in close agre-
ement with Luther, wrote the *Augsburg Confession*, which
represents the fundamental doctrine of every Lutheran
church to this day. Luther himself honed his theological
teachings in the *Schmalkaldic Articles (Die Schmalkal-
dischen Artikel)* of 1538.

In order to consolidate the nascent Protestant Church,
the new forms of service had to be disseminated to the
pastors. In 1526 Luther completed *The German Mass
and Order of Divine Service (Deutsche Messe und Ordnung des Gottesdiensts)*, emphasizing that he regarded
it as an example rather than an order to be enforced on
all. He took a similar line with the *Baptism Booklet (Tauf-
büchlein)* and the *Marriage Booklet (Traubüchlein)*.

Luther pursued his school reforms with great vigor, as
exemplified by *A Sermon on Keeping Children in School*

(*Eine Predigt, dass man Kinder zur Schule halten solle*). His initiative for economic reform also continued with his *Admonition to the Clergy that they Preach Against Usury* (*An die Pfarrherren, wider den Wucher zu predigen*). But here it becomes apparent that even Luther no longer believed in a complete abolition of usury. Consequently he tells pastors to keep pursuing the issue for the sake of their own consciences, even if without success.

The attitude of the local ruler played a decisive role in deciding the fate of the Reformation in German territories. In a richly detailed *woodcut* (*Fig. 78*) made after Luther's death, Pankratius Kempff shows the battle between the enemies of Christ, in this case the Church of Rome and a Turk, and the supporters of the Reformation, among whom we find Luther, John Huss, Melanchthon, Caspar Cruciger, the elector of Saxony, and the landgrave of Hesse.

Two other decisive defenders of the Reformation were Duke Ernest of Brunswick-Lüneburg-Celle, who studied in Wittenberg from 1512 to 1515, and Duke Ernest of Brunswick-Grubenhagen. Their *portraits by the Cranach workshop* (*Fig. 79, 80* ▶) were originally probably part of a larger gallery of Protestant rulers

■ *Fig. 78   A Song, O Lord, Keep Us To Your Word, Pancratius Kempff, colored woodcut, c. 1550*

■ *Fig. 79 Ernest the Confessor, Duke of Brunswick-Lüneburg-Celle, Lucas Cranach the Elder (workshop), oil on wood, sixteenth century, excerpt*

■ *Fig. 80 Duke Ernest of Brunswick-Grubenhagen, Lucas Cranach the Elder (workshop), oil on wood, sixteenth century, excerpt*

"We are beggars: this is true. "
    Luther in a note written shortly before his death in 1546

Luther's Death and his Lasting Legacy

All his life Luther felt very attached to his home region, the county of Mansfeld. When the ruling counts fell into disagreement over the distribution of mining revenues and the founding of a new school, they asked Luther to settle the dispute. Although feeling physically unwell, he agreed to their request in January 1546. So it was that on February 18, 1546, Luther's life ended where it began, in Eisleben.

Luther's physical decline is recorded in a *pen-and-ink drawing (Fig. 81)* stuck inside a Latin gospel book, which was also used as a family album and contains entries by Luther, Bugenhagen, and Melanchthon. Unlike the semi-official portraits by the Cranach workshop, this drawing clearly shows his thinning hair and the cataract on his left eye.

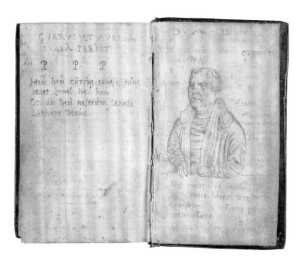

■ *Fig. 81   Martin Luther in the last year of his life, Johann Reiffenstein, pen-and-ink drawing, 1545, glued into a copy of The Gospels according to Matthew and Mark (Paris: Robert Stephanus, 1541)*

The Saxon elector had the body taken to Wittenberg against the will of the counts of Mansfeld. A drawing of Luther's corpse made before it left Eisleben served as a

■ *Fig. 82 Luther on his Deathbed, oil on wood, seventeenth century*

model for a *deathbed portrait (Fig. 82),* of which many copies were made.

At the funeral in Wittenberg's Castle Church, recorded in a *woodcut of 1557 (Fig. 83),* Johann Bugenhagen held the funeral sermon for his friend, not concealing his concern for the future of the Protestant Church after Luther's death. News of Luther's death spread rapidly and brought forth a myriad of printed reactions, including *A Good Christian Song of the Honorable Dr. Martin Luther (Ein schönes christliches Lied von dem ehrwürdigen Herren D. Martin Luther, Fig. 84)* with the striking portrait woodcut. Luther's tomb was discovered in 1892 during

■ *Fig. 83 Luther's Funeral in Wittenberg Castle Church, colored woodcut, 1557*

■ *Fig. 84 Johann Friedrich Petsch, A Good Christian Song of the Honorable Dr. Martin Luther (Wittenberg: Georg Rhau, 1546)*

■ *Fig. 85 Handle from Luther's coffin, wrought iron, 1546*

building work in the Castle Church. Ignoring the Kaiser's prohibition, two building officials removed a *handle from Luther's coffin* (◄ *Fig. 85*), which has been kept in the Luther House since 1913.

The exhibition room is dominated by the remains of the passageway to Luther's study in a tower in the now-demolished city walls, whose foundations can be seen as you enter the museum. The passageway was found in 1982, but the foundations of the tower did not come to light until 2000.

Luther's primary legacy is his prose, whose influence is still felt today. The most significant work is his *Bible translation (Fig. 86)*, which shaped the development of the German language like no other book.

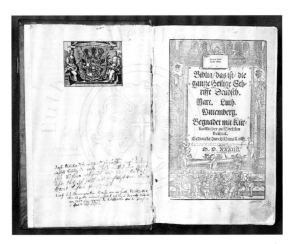

■ *Fig. 86   Martin Luther,* The Entire Holy Scripture, *German (Wittenberg: Hans Lufft, 1534)*

Although his translation of the New Testament was published in 1522, it was another twelve years before the first complete edition of the Holy Scriptures went to print in Luther's rendition. The book became the "bestseller" of the Reformation, and revised versions are still in use in Protestant churches today.

Second place is taken by Luther's hymns. *Klug's Songbook (Das Klug'sche Gesangbuch, Fig. 87* ►*)*, named after the printer, contains the first printed version of his probably best-known hymn, "A Mighty Fortress Is Our

■ *Plate 5   Law and Grace, Lucas Cranach the Elder, Lucas Cranach the Younger, oil on wood, 1551, on loan from the State of Saxony-Anhalt*

■ *Fig. 87 Martin Luther, A Mighty Fortress Is Our God, from Spiritual Hymns in Wittenberg, second edition (Wittenberg: Joseph Klug, 1533)*

God." Unlike the expensive Bibles, the small-format hymnbooks were so cheap that even ordinary people could afford to replace them if they got lost or destroyed.

As a result, hardly any copies of the early hymnbooks have been preserved. In fact, not one single first edition copy has survived, and from the second edition only the exhibited example.

The same applies to the *Prayer Booklet (Betbüchlein)*. Alongside his Bible translation and catechisms, this collection was one of Luther's most successful publications. First published in 1522, thirty-seven editions were printed before his death. The exhibited copy from Nuremberg is one of only two to survive from that edition.

Law and Grace (◀ *Plate 5, pp. 101–102)* is a treatment of Luther's theology painted in the early 1550s. It cannot be determined whether by the older or the younger Cranach. The clear differentiation of the Bible stories, with the Old Testament on the left, the Gospels on the right, corresponds to Luther's insistence on the distinction of law and gospel as the essence of his theology. The Latin Bible extracts that refer to different parts of the painting serve to underline this distinction.

This pictorial representation of biblical theology was in keeping with Luther's ideas that pictures should be used primarily for educational purposes. The small format and the high quality of the work suggest that it was made for a rich private client.

Notes from german sources

p. 9:   Friedensburg, Walter:
Geschichte der Universität
Wittenberg, Halle/Saale 1917, 45

p. 21:   WA 4, 637, 40

p. 25:   WA 1, 236, 23f.

p. 37:   WA 6, 404, 11f.

p. 47:   WA 7, 838, 7–9

p. 57:   WABr 2, 412, 22f.

p. 63:   WA 15, 219, 1–9

p. 75:   WA 10 II, 276, 19f.

p. 89:   WA 6, 131, 16

p. 93:   WATR 1, 72, 33

p. 97:   WA 48, 241

Catalog

List of Abbreviations

B. – Bartsch, Adam von. 1803–1821. Vol. 7 of Le
Peintre Graveur. 21 vols. Vienna.
Benzing –Benzing, Josef, and Helmut Claus.
1989 and 1994. Lutherbibliographie: Verzeichnis
der gedruckten Schriften Martin Luthers bis zu
dessen Tod. 2 vols. Baden-Baden.
Claus/Pegg – Claus, H., and M. A. Pegg (comps.).
1982. Ergänzungen zur Bibliographie der zeit-
genössischen Lutherdrucke: Im Anschluss an
die Lutherbibliographie Josef Benzings. Gotha.
Gebhart – Gebhart, Hans. 1924. Die Münzen und
Medaillen der Stadt Donauwörth. Halle/Saale.
Götz – Götz, Christian Jacob. 1827. Beiträge zum
Groschen-Cabinet. Dresden.
H. – Hollstein, Friedrich Wilhelm Heinrich (founder). 1954ff. German Engravings, Etchings and
Woodcuts ca. 1400–1700. Amsterdam. Cited
here: Vol. 6. Karel G. Boon and Robert W. Schel-
ler, eds. 1961. Cranach-Drusse.
Habich – Habich, Georg. 1929–1934. Die deut-
schen Schaumünzen des XVI. Jahrhunderts.
Munich.
Harms – Harms, Wolfgang, ed. 1997. Deutsche
illustrierte Flugblätter des 16. und 17. Jahrhunderts: Die Sammlung der Herzog August Biblio-
thek in Wolfenbüttel. Vol. 2. Tübingen: Historica.

Harms/Rattay – Harms, Wolfgang (ed.) and
Beate Rattay (comp.). 1983. Illustrierte Flugblätter
aus den Jahrhunderten der Reformation und der
Glaubenskämpfe. Coburg.
J. – Jahn, Johannes and Marianne Bernhard
(eds.), ed. 1972. Lucas Cranach d. Ä.–Das
gesamte graphische Werk: Mit Exempeln aus
dem graphischen Werk Lucas Cranach d. J. und
der Cranach-Werkstatt. Munich.
Juncker – Juncker, Christian. 1706. Das guldene
und silberne Ehren-Gedächtnis des teuren
Gottes-Lehrers D. Martini Lutheri. Frankfurt and
Leipzig.
KF – Koepplin, Dieter, and Tilman Falk. 1974.
Lucas Cranach: Gemälde, Zeichnungen, Druck-
graphik. 2 vols. Basle and Stuttgart: Kunstmu-
seum Basel, 1974–76.
Krug – Krug, Gerhard. 1974. Die meißnisch-säch-
sischen Groschen 1338–1500. Berlin.
Schnee – Schnee, Gemot. 1982. Sächsische
Taler 1500–1800. Frankfurt/Main.

Schulten – Schulten, Wolfgang. 1974. Deutsche
Münzen aus der Zeit Karls V. Frankfurt/Main.
Slg. Whiting – Sammlung Prof. Robert B. Whiting,
Philadelphia. Martin Luther und die Reformation
auf Münzen und Medaillen. Auction catalog of
April 19–20, 1983, Spink & Son Ltd., Zurich and
C. E. Bullowa. Philadelphia.
VD 16 – Verzeichnis der im deutschen Sprach-
bereich erschienenen Drucke des 16. Jahrhun-
derts: 1983ff. Stuttgart.
WA – D. Martin Luthers Werke: Kritische Gesamt-
ausgabe. 1883ff. Weimar.

Biographical Tour
Exhibits as per September 5, 2003

Martin Luther's Path
to Wittenberg, 1483–1508

Statue of St. Anne
Swabia
Limewood, carved, c. 1520
570 mm x 380 mm x 220 mm
Classification number: P 80

View of Wittenberg
Three-block woodcut, 1536–46
265 mm x 1,095 mm (300 mm x 1,118 mm)
Classification number: CGH 497Luther Memorial
Foundation/C. G. Holzhausen Foundation

Model of the city of Wittenberg around 1500
Acrylic glass, wood, 2003

Wittenberg – University Town and Electoral
Residence

Prince Elector Frederick III
Lucas Cranach the Elder (workshop)
Oil on beech, 1532
132 mm x 120 mm (267 mm x 255 mm)
Classification number: G 22

Joust
Lucas Cranach the Elder
Woodcut, 1506/09
Reprint from the original block, early 17th century
261 mm x 374 mm (264 mm x 376 mm)
Classification number: fl XX 11695
Private loan
H. 116, J. 130ff, KF 108

Double page showing reliquaries
Lucas Cranach the Elder
in: Georg Spalatin and Lucas Cranach the Elder:
Die Zeigung des hochlobwürdigen Heiltums (Wit-
tenberg Book of Relics). Wittenberg: Symphorian
Reinhart, 1509
Classification number: ss 3579
205 x 310 mm (when opened)
On loan from the State of Saxony-Anhalt
VD 16 Z 250, H. 96, Z. AI 1-119, J. 461-544, KF 96-
101

Reliquary
Tyrol/Northern Italy
Copper, gilt, c. 1520
460 mm x 133 mm x 146 mm
Classification number: K 287

St. Anthony
Lucas Cranach the Elder (workshop)
Oil on wood, c. 1520
455 mm x 135 mm (510 mm x 189 mm)
Classification number: G 158 (LG)
On loan from the State of Saxony-Anhalt

St. Sebastian
Lucas Cranach the Elder (workshop)
Oil on wood, c. 1520
455 mm x 137 mm (510 mm x 190 mm)
Classification number: G 159 (LG)
On loan from the State of Saxony-Anhalt

Disc candlestick
Brass, 16th century
585 mm x 180 mm
Classification number: K 290

Censer
Cast brass, 18th century
150 mm x 260 mm x 100 mm
Classification number: K 277

Corbel from the former Franciscan church
in Wittenberg
Sandstone, 14th/15th century
395 mm x 320 mm x 590 mm

Luther's Reformational Discovery

Luther's marginalia
in: Collected works of St. Jerome of Stridon.
Vols. 3 and 4. Edited by Erasmus of Rotterdam
(Hieronymus, Sophronius Eusebius: Omnium
Operum divi Eusebii Hieronymi Stridonensis . . .
Tomus Tertius/Quartus . . . Des. Erasmi Rotero-
dami . . . Opera . . . Emendat . .) Basle: Johann
Froben, 1516
On loan from the Wittenberg Preachers Seminary

Christ on the Cross
Lucas Cranach the Younger
Oil on canvas, 1571
2,510 mm x 1,580 mm (2,720 mm x 1,805 mm)
On loan from the Wittenberg Preachers Seminary

Parchment of the Monastery of the Hermits of
St. Augustine in Wittenberg on the sale of an
annual tithe in the possession of the monastery
to the Collegiate Chapter of All Saints (Castle
Church)
Wittenberg, May 5, 1509, 440 mm x 390 mm
Classification number: Urk./844,

Seal of Wittenberg University 1503–14
Silver, 16th century
78 mm x 46 mm x 30 mm
Classification number: K 14

Seal of Wittenberg University as of 1514
Lucas Cranach the Elder
Bronze, copper, steel (replica)
Diameter 40 mm
Classification number: K 142

Luther with doctoral cap
Daniel Hopfer
Etching, 1523
188 mm x 156 mm (237 mm x 171mm)
Call number: fl III a 9366

**The Ninety-five Theses–the Beginnings of
the Reformation, 1517**

Indulgence chest
Sheet iron bound with iron straps
Wrought lid with five locks, 16th century
420 mm x 750 mm x 470 mm
Classification number: K 372

Caricature of Johann Tetzel selling indulgences
Woodcut, 1617
136 mm x 160 mm (269 mm x 161 mm)
Classification number: fl IX 3396

Harms/Rattay p. 14f.
Without Indulgence from Rome One Can Still
be Saved (Ohn' Ablaß von Rom kann man wohl
selig werden)
Augsburg: Melchior Ramminger, 1521
Classification number: Ag 4° 191 a
VD 16 O 527

Writ of indulgence
For one hundred days in purgatory, issued by
eighteen cardinals for visitors of the Lady Cha-
pel in the parish of St. James in Puchbach, diocese of Salzburg
Rome, August 31, 1492
690 mm x 900 mm
Classification number: Urk./4605

The Great Joust
Jakob Binck
Copperplate engraving, 16th century
(440 mm x 578 mm)
Classification number: grfl XIV 8860

Pope Leo X
Tobias Stimmer after Raphael
Woodcut, 1573
125 mm x 110 mm (200 mm x 165 mm)
Classification number: 4° XXVII 3562

Cardinal Albrecht of Brandenburg
Lucas Cranach the Elder
Copperplate engraving, 1520
171 mm x 115 mm (202 mm x 140 mm)
Classification number: fl XV 3541
B. 4, H. 2, J. 211, KF 34

Letter of indulgence
Blank letter of indulgence from the campaign of
Archbishop Albrecht of Mainz and Magdeburg
for the building of St. Peter's in Rome
Parchment, 1515
145 mm x 189 mm
Classification number: Urk./3213

Donauwörth
Thaler, 1548
Donauwörth mint
Mintmaster Balthasar Hundertpfund
Silver, 41 mm, 28.5 g
Classification number: M 60
Gebhart 113, Schulten 757

Electorate of Saxony
John the Steadfast
Thaler, no year (1525–32)
Zwickau mint
Silver, 40 mm, 29.0 g
Classification number: M 91
Schulten 3051, Schnee 54

Electorate of Saxony
August I
Thaler, 1564
Dresden mint
Mintmaster Hans Biener
Silver, 40 mm, 28.8 g
Classification number: M 93
Schnee 713

Electorate of Saxony and Duchy of Saxony
Frederick III the Wise, Albrecht, and designated
Elector John
Saxonian "Schreckenberger" or "Engelgroschen"
coins, no year (1498–1500)
Annaberg mint
Mintmasters Heinrich Stein and Augustin Horn
Silver, 28 mm, 4.4 g
Classification number: M 96
Krug 2132

Electorate of Saxony, Duchy of Saxony and
Landgravate of Thuringia
Ernest, Duke Albrecht, and Duke William III
Saxonian "Spitzgroschen" coin 1475
Zwickau mint
Silver, 21 mm, 1.5 g
Classification number: MH M 340
Krug 1521

Margravate of Brandenburg-Ansbach and Bran-
denburg-Kulmbach
Frederick I and Sigismund
Gold florin, no year (15th century)
Schwabach mint
Gold, 23 mm, 3.2 g
Call number: M 22
Friedberg 459

Martin Luther's pulpit
Limewood and oak, carpentered, carved, painted, second half of the 15th century
2, 465 mm x 890 mm x 900 mm
On loan from the Protestant parish of Wittenberg City Church

Luther as monk
Lucas Cranach the Elder
Copperplate engraving, 1520
Reprint from the original plate, c. 1570–90
(141 mm x 97 mm)
Classification number: fl IIIa 208
B. 5, H. 6 III (of III), J. 207, KF 35

Martin Luther
The Ninety-five Theses (Disputatio pro declara-
tione virtutis indulgentiarum). October 31, 1517
Basle: Adam Petri, 1517
Classification number: ss 2183
Benzing 89, VD 16 L 4457, WA 1. 231 C

Martin Luther
A Sermon on Indulgences and Grace (Ein Ser-
mon von Ablass und Gnade)
Leipzig: Wolfgang Stöckel, 1518
Classification number: Ag 4° 185 g
Benzing 94, VD 16 L 6272, WA 1. 240 D

Martin Luther
A Sermon on Indulgences and Grace (Ein Ser-
mon von Ablass und Gnade)
Wittenberg: Johann Rhau-Grunenberg, 1518
Classification number: Ag 4° 185 f
Benzing 91, Claus/Pegg 91 a, VD 16 L 6278, WA
1. 240 B

Martin Luther
A Sermon on Indulgences and Grace (Ein Ser-
mon von Ablass und Gnade)
Basle: Pamphilus Gengenbach, 1518
Classification number: Ag 4° 185 h
Benzing 101, VD 16 L 6267, WA 1. 241 L

Martin Luther
A Sermon on Indulgences and Grace (Ein Ser-
mon von Ablass und Gnade)
Nuremberg: Jobst Gutknecht, 1518
Classification number: Kn D 1
Benzing 97, VD 16 L 6274, WA 1. 238 G

Martin Luther
A Sermon on Indulgences and Grace (Ein Ser-
mon von Ablass und Gnade)
Leipzig: Wolfgang Stöckel, 1520
Classification number: Ag 4° 188 d
Benzing 109, VD 16 L 6288, WA 1. 242 T

Martin Luther
Explanation of the Sermon on Papal Indulgen-
ces and Grace (Eine Freiheit des Sermons
päpstlichen Ablass und Gnade belangend)
Augsburg: Jörg Nadler, 1520
Classification number: Ag 4° 188 g
Benzing 190, VD 16 L 4750, WA 1. 381 J

Martin Luther
A Sermon on Indulgences and Grace (Ein Ser-
mon von Ablass und Gnade)
Wittenberg: Johann Rhau-Grunenberg, 1520
Classification number: Ag 4° 188 h
Benzing 112, VD 16 L 6289, WA 1. 242 W

Ten Commandments panel
Lucas Cranach the Elder (workshop)
Oil on wood, 1516
(1,585 mm x 3,530 mm)
On loan from the City of Wittenberg

**The Audition in Augsburg and the Leipzig
Disputation, 1518–1519**

Luther before Cajetan
Colored woodcut, 1557
67 mm x 107 mm (78 mm x 113 mm)
from: Rabus, Ludwig: Historien der Heyligen
Außerwölten Gottes Zeugen
Strasbourg: Samuel Emmel, 1557
Call number: 4° XII a 1581b

Martin Luther
The Deeds of the Augustinian Brother M. Luther
Before the Papal Legate at Augsburg (Acta Fra-
tris M. Lutheri Augustiniani apud Legatum Apo-
stolicum Augustae)
Leipzig: Valentin Schumann, 1518
Classification number: Ag 4° 185 t
Benzing 237, VD 16 L 3642, WA 2. 3 D

The Leipzig Disputation
Colored woodcut, 1557
72 mm x 107 mm (76 mm x 113 mm)
from: Rabus, Ludwig: Historien.
Classification number: 4° XII a 1581c

Duke George of Saxony
Lucas Cranach the Younger
Woodcut, c. 1562
160 mm x 112 mm (175 mm x 132 mm)
from: Agricola, Johannes: Wahrhafte Bildnis etli-
cher hochlöblicher Fürsten and Herren. Wittenberg: Gabriel Schnellboltz, 1562
Classification number: 4° XLIV 5218

Luther as monk
Hans Weiditz II
Woodcut, c. 1522
148 mm x 117 mm (169 mm x 121 mm)
from: Luther, Martin: Vom ehelichen Leben.
Augsburg: Heinrich Steiner 1523
Benzing 1250, VD 16 L 7034, WA 10,2. 270 L
Classification number: 4° II a 223

Andreas Bodenstein Karlstadt
Etching, 16th century
110 mm x 70 mm (115 mm x 80 mm)
Classification number: 4° XXIII 2559

Martin Luther
A Sermon Held at the Castle in Leipzig on the
Day of Sts. Peter and Paul, Matthew 16:13–19,
June 29, 1519 (Ein Sermon gepredigt zu Leipzig
auf dem Schloss am Tage Petri and Pauli Mat-
thäus 16, 13–19. 29. Juni 1519)
Leipzig: Wolfgang Stöckel, 1520

Classification number: Ag 4° 188 u
Benzing 403, VD 16 L 6197, WA 2. 242 F

Hourglass
Carved beech and oak, painted cardboard,
glass, gold leaf, 17th century
750 mm x 305 mm x 200 mm
On loan from the City of Wittenberg

Lectern
Wood, painted on a chalk background, with
punched rhombic pattern, gold leaf, washed
brush drawings on a gilt background in five of
the medallions, 17th century
480 mm x 540 mm 370 mm
On loan from the Protestant parish of Wittenberg City Church

John Huss
Jürgen Creutzberger after Erhard Schön
Woodcut, 16th century
428 mm x 357 mm (565 mm x 380 mm)
Call number: grfl I 69a

**Key Reformatory Writings and the Burning
of Church Law, 1520**

Martin Luther
On Good Works (Von den guten Werken)
Wittenberg: Melchior Lotter the Younger, 1520
Classification number: Ag 4° 190 a
Benzing 635, VD 16 L 7142, WA 6. 197 C

Martin Luther
A Prelude on the Babylonian Captivity of the
Church (De captivitate Babylonica ecclesiae
praeludium)
Wittenberg: Melchior Lotter the Younger, 1520,
first edition
Classification number: Ag 4° 191 c
Benzing 704, VD 16 L 4189, WA 6. 489 A

Martin Luther
An Open Letter to the Christian Nobility of the
German Nation Concerning the Reform of the
Christian Estate (An den christlichen Adel deut-
scher Nation von des christlichen Standes Bes-
serung)
Wittenberg: Melchior Lotter the Younger, 1520,
first edition
Classification number: Ag 4° 189 f
Benzing 683, VD 16 L 3758, WA 6. 397 A

Martin Luther
On Christian Liberty (Von der Freiheit eines Chri-
stenmenschen)
Wittenberg: Johann Rhau-Grunenberg, 1520,
first edition
Classification number: Kn D 69
Benzing 734, VD 16 L 7189, WA 7. 15 A

Pope Leo X
Papal Bull Against Luther and his Followers
(Bulla contra errores Martini Lutheri et sequa-
cium)
Rome: Jacobus Mazochius, 1520
Classification number: ss 3519

Pope Leo X
The Bull under the Name of Pope Leo X Against
Excommunicated Doctor Martinus Luther, Trans-
lated into German by Georg Spalatin (Die ver-
deutschte Bulle, unter dem Namen des Pap-
stes Leo X. wider Doktor Martinus Luther ausge-
gangen)
Leipzig: Valentin Schumann, 1520
Classification number: Kn A 76/564
VD 16 K 283

Luther's Books Are Burned
Woodcut, 1524
130 mm x 105 mm (155 mm x 130 mm)
Classification number: 4° XII a 1397

Luther Burns the Papal Bull
Colored woodcut, 1557
71 mm x 72 mm (75 mm x 77 mm)
from: Rabus, Ludwig: Historien
Classification number: 4 ° XII a 1581d

Johannes Fanckel
Collected Writings and Conclusions on the Cle-
mentines and the Extravagantes (Two Canoni-
cal Collections) (Summarium textuale et con-
clusiones Clementinarum et Extravagantium)
Cologne: Johannes Koelhoff the Elder, October
27, 1484
Classification number: ss 2166

Angelus de Clavasio
The Angelic Summa on Cases of Conscience
(Summa angelica de casibus conscientiae)
Nuremberg: Anton Koberger, August 28, 1488
Classification number: ss 2146

Johann Eck
Chrysopassus
Augsburg: Johann Miller, November 1514
Call number: ss 3608
VD 16 E 305

Johann Eck
An Apology for the Council of Constance Where
John Huss was Burnt Despite Papal Safe Con-
duct and Oath (Des heiligen Konzils zu Kon-
stanz Entschuldigung, sie haben Johannes Hus
wider päpstlich Geleit und Eid verbrannt)
Leipzig: Martin Landsberg, 1520
Classification number: Ag 4° 268 f
VD 16 E 379

Johann Eck
A Reply to Those Things that Philipp Melancht-
hon Falsely Argued at the Theological Disputa-
tion in Leipzig (Excusatio ad ea, quae falso sibi
Philippus Melanchthon super Theologica dispu-
tatione Lipsica adscripsit)
Leipzig: Martin Landsberg, 1519
Classification number: Ag 4° 268 e
VD 16 E 373

Hieronymus Emser
An den Stier zu Wittenberg (Martin Luther) (To
the Wittenberg Bull)
Leipzig: Martin Landsberg, 1520
Classification number: Kn B 51/347
VD 16 E 1082

Pope Leo X
Papal Bull Against Luther and his Followers
(Bulla contra errores Martini Lutheri et sequa-
cium)
Strasbourg: Johann Schott, 1520
Classification number: Kn A 170/1012
VD 16 K 277

Martin Luther
Why the Books of the Pope and his Followers
Are Burned by Dr. Martin Luther (Warum des
Papstes und seiner Jünger Bücher von D. M.
Luther verbrannt sind)
Wittenberg: Johann Rhau-Grunenberg, 1520
Classification number: Ag 4° 190 r
Benzing 785, VD 16 L 7366, WA 7. Ba-c

The Ascension of Christ – the Descent of the
Pope into Hell
Lucas Cranach the Elder (workshop)
in: Passional Christi und Antichristi. Wittenberg:
Johann Rhau-Grunenberg, 1521
Classification number: ss 40
VD 16 L 5585, H. 66a-z, J. 557-583, KF 218

Worms–Before Emperor and Empire, 1521

Folding chair
Northern foothills of the Alps or Tyrol
Beech, early 16th century
865 mm x 677 mm x 600 mm
Call number: K 274

Coconut goblet
Christoff Ritterle
Nuremberg
Cast silver, gilt, chased, engraved, c. 1560
305 mm x 95 mm
Classification number: K 289

View of Worms
Franz Hogenberg
Colored etching, 1593
110 mm x 470 mm (133 mm x 497 mm)
Classification number: grflVII 8100

Luther at the Imperial Diet in Worms
Colored woodcut, 1557
73 mm x 107 mm (78 mm x 111 mm)
from: Rabus, Ludwig: Historien
Classification number: 4° XIIa 1581 e

Habit of an Augustinian monk
Allegedly worn by Luther
Woolen fabric, 16th century
1,380 mm x 620 mm
Classification number: K 373

Emperor Charles V
Minna Pfüller after Christoph Amberger
Oil on canvas, second half of the 19th century
630 mm x 485 mm (770 mm x 615 mm)
Classification number: G 125

Luther with doctoral cap
Lucas Cranach the Elder
Oil on wood (copied onto canvas), c. 1520
260 mm x 180 mm
Classification number: G 163 (LG)
On loan from the State of Saxony-Anhalt / East-
German Savings Bank Foundation in the State
of Saxony-Anhalt, and the Wittenberg Savings
Bank

Emperor Charles V
Edict Against Martin Luther's Writings and Tea-
chings (Edikt wider Martin Luthers Bücher und
Lehre)
Nuremberg: Hieronymus Höltzel, 1524
Classification number: Kn A 9/53
VD 16 D 929

Doctor Martin Luther's Public Hearing at the
Imperial Diet in Worms, his Words and the
Reply (Doktor Martini Luthers öffentliches Verhör
zu Worms im Reichstag, Rede und Widerrede)
Augsburg: Melchior Ramminger, 1521
Classification number: ss 3520
Benzing 930, VD 16 L 3655, WA 7. 864 P

Hans Wallser
A Report on How Doctor Martin Luther First
Found Out about this Scandalous Traffic in

Indulgences (Ein Bericht wie Doctor Martini
Luther als erster hinter diesen schweren Ablas-
shandel gekommen sei)
Augsburg: Melchior Ramminger, 1521
Classification number: Kn A 278/1946
VD 16 W 914

An Announcement Concerning Dr. Martin
Luther's Appearance before the Imperial Diet in
Worms, his Questioning by His Majesty the
Emperor in Person, and the Consequences
(Eine Anzeigung wie D. Martinus Luther zu
Worms auf dem Reichstag eingefahren durch
Kaiserliche Majestät in eigner Person verhört
und mit ihm darauf gehandelt)
Augsburg: Melchior Ramminger, 1521
Classification number: Kn 31/263
Benzing 931, VD 16 A 3024, WA 7. 883 Q

Martin Luther
Letter to Emperor Charles V
Friedberg, April 28, 1521
292 mm x 426 mm
Classification number: I5/1387

Luther at Wartburg Castle, 1521–1522

Luther as Knight George before Worms
Heinrich Göding the Elder
Etching, 1598
263 mm x 185 mm (270 mm x 186 mm)
Classification number: fl III 467

Luther as St. Jerome in his Study
Wolfgang Stuber after Albrecht Dürer
Copperplate engraving, c. 1580
(136 mm x 126 mm)
Classification number: 4° IV 469

Martin Luther
The German New Testament (September Testa-
ment) (Das Neue Testament deutsch [Septem-
bertestament])
Wittenberg: Melchior Lotter the Younger, Sep-
tember 1522
Classification number: Kn K 1
VD 16 B 4318

Candlestick
Germany, c. 1500
Iron
102 mm x 60 mm
Classification number: K 303

Martin Luther
Advent Postil (Adventspostille)
Wittenberg: Johann Rhau-Grunenberg, 1522,
first edition
Classification number: Ag 4° 195 c
Benzing 1064, VD 16 L 3924,
WA 10,1,2. XIV A

**The Wittenberg Movement and Luther's
Return, 1522**

View of Wittenberg
Cranach workshop
Colored woodcut, c. 1558
(130 mm x 230 mm)
Classification number: fl X 8348

An Admonition for the Young
Woodcut, first half of the 16th century
(373 mm x 287 mm)
Classification number: fl XX 11093

Receipt from the Wittenberg common chest
Certificate, December 6, 1531
225 mm x 214 mm
Classification number: Urk./4637

A Commendable Statute for the Princely City of
Wittenberg (Eine löbliche Ordnung der fürstli-
chen Stadt Wittenberg)
Augsburg: Melchior Ramminger, 1522
Classification number: Kn A 117/682
VD 16 W 3697

Martin Luther
Ordinance of a Common Chest (Ordnung
eines gemeinen Kastens. Ratschlag, wie die
geistlichen Güter zu handeln sind)
Wittenberg: Lucas Cranach and Christian
Döring, 1523, first edition
Classification number: Ag 4° 198 p
Benzing 1607, VD 16 L 5570, WA 12. 9 A

Johann Eberlin
How it Be Dangerous if a Priest Has No Wife
(Wie gar gefährlich sei, so ein Priester kein Ehe-
weib hat)
Augsburg: Melchior Ramminger, 1522
Classification number: Ag 4° 242 dVD 16 E 156

Martin Luther
On the Right and Power of a Christian Congre-
gation or Parish to Judge all Doctrine and to
Appoint and Dismiss Teachers, for Reasons
Based on Holy Scripture (Dass eine christliche
Versammlung oder Gemeine Recht und
Macht habe, alle Lehre zu urteilen und Lehrer zu
berufen, ein- und abzusetzen. Grund und Ursa-
che aus der Schrift)
Wittenberg: Lucas Cranach and Christian
Döring, 1523, first edition
Classification number: Kn K 66
Benzing 1569, VD 16 L 4290, WA 11. 402 A

Common chest of the city of Wittenberg
Chest with three separate locks
Iron, c. 1520
590 mm x 1,200 mm x 640 mm
On loan from the City of Wittenberg

Double pietà
Wood, carved, 16th century
1,240 mm x 640 mm x 780 mm
Classification number: P 82a

Andreas Bodenstein Karlstadt
On the Removal of Images (Von Abtuung der
Bilder)
Wittenberg: Nickel Schirlentz, 1522
Classification number: Kn A 11/69
VD 16 B 6214

Martin Luther
Eight Lenten Sermons at Wittenberg (Acht Ser-
mone D. M. Luthers von ihm gepredigt zu Wit-
tenberg in der Fasten)
(Invocavit sermons of March 9–16, 1522)
Augsburg: Heinrich Steiner, 1523
Classification number: Ag 4° 200l
Benzing 50, VD 16 L 3632, WA 10.3. LXXIV B

Reforms in the Parish, 1522–1525

Chasuble with image of the Virgin Mary
Silk velvet, embroidered, 15th/16th century
1,140 mm x 960 mm

On loan from the Protestant parish of Zwochau

Special Missal
Strasbourg: Reinhard Beck, August 1518
Classification number: ss 3522
VD 16 M 5629

Communion cup
Martin Baumgärtner
Silver, gilt, chased, 16th century/1636
218 mm x 125 mm
Classification number: K 275

Martin Luther
On the Order of Service in the Parish (Von Ord-
nung des Gottesdiensts in der Gemeinde)
Wittenberg: Lucas Cranach and Christian
Döring, 1523, first edition
Classification number: Ag 4° 198 h
Benzing 1615, VD 16 L 7305, WA 12. 32 A

Small Spiritual Songbook for Tenor (Geistliches
Gesangbüchlein Tenor)
Wittenberg: Joseph Klug, 1524
Classification number: ss 2181
Benzing 3539, VD 16 L 4776, WA 35. 315 A

Luther Delivering a Sermon
Woodcut, 16th century
135 mm x 128 mm (208 mm x 144 mm)
Classification number: 4° XII a 1367

Luther and Huss Administering the Sacrament
in Both Ways
Cranach workshop
Woodcut, c. 1550
(277 mm x 241 mm)
Classification number: fl VIII 1104

Corn Extortion
Daniel Hopfer, 1534
Copperplate engraving, 17th century
(201 mm x 276 mm)
Classification number: fl XX 8816

Members of the Roman Church Complain
about Luther
Sebald Beham
Woodcut, c. 1524
(151 mm x 262 mm)
Classification number: fl IX 8407

The Monastic Life of Luxury: An Allegory
Sebald Beham
Woodcut, 1521
94 mm x 162 mm (102 mm x 168 mm)
Classification number: fl IX 8928

Martin Luther
On Commerce and Usury (Von Kaufshandlung
und Wucher)
Nuremberg: Hans Hergot, 1524
Classification number: Ag 4° 202 x
Benzing 1943, VD 16 L 7276, WA 15. 285 D

Martin Luther
To the Councilmen of All Cities in Germany That
They Establish and Maintain Christian Schools
(An die Ratherren aller Städte deutschen Lan-
des, dass sie christliche Schulen aufrichten und
halten sollen)
Wittenberg: Lucas Cranach and Christian
Döring, 1524
Classification number: Ag 4° 202 r
Benzing 1875, VD 16 L 3800, WA 15. 15 A

The Peasants' Revolt and Thomas Müntzer, 1525

Thomas Müntzer
Christoffel van Sichem
Etching, 1608
171 mm x 123 mm (267 mm x 164 mm)
from: Historische beschrijvinge ende affbeel-
dinge der voorneemste Hooftketteren..., Amsterdam, 1608
Classification number: 4° XXIII 3307

Diepold Peringer
A Sermon by Peasants at Wöhrd near Nurem-
berg on Human Free Will Ein Sermon, gepredi-
get vom Bauern zu Wöhrd bei Nürnberg, von
dem freien Willen des Menschen)
Erfurt: Wolfgang Stürmer, 1524
Classification number: Ag 4° 275 Gamma
VD 16 P 1408

The Fundamental and Just Demands of the
Peasantry (Die gründlichen und rechten
Hauptartikel aller Bauernschaft)
Zwickau: Jörg Gastel, 1525
Classification number: Kn A 341/2404
VD 16 G 3563

Knife for self-defense
Switzerland or southern Germany
Wrought iron, early 16th century
438 mm x 35 mm
Classification number: K 281

Halberd
Germany or Switzerland
Wrought iron, wood, c. 1520
1,410 mm x 255 mm x 40 mm
Classification number: K 282

Partisan or spear
Italy
Wrought iron, wood, 16th century
2,435 mm x 70 mm x 40 mm
Classification number: K 283

Halberd
Germany or Switzerland
Wrought iron, wood, mid-16th century
2,270 mm x 245 mm x 35 mm
Classification number: K 284

Halberd
Styria
Wrought iron, wood, 16th century
2,095 mm x 250 mm x 30 mm
Classification number: K 285

Halberd
Styria
Wrought iron, wood, 16th century
1,930 mm x 255 mm
Classification number: K 286

Cuirass and closed helmet
Iron, etched, c. 1520
475 mm x 375 mm x 150 mm (breastplate),
335 mm x 220 mm x 340 mm (closed helmet)
On loan from the City of Eisleben

Gun barrel
Cast iron, 16th century
1,050 mm x 160 mm
On loan from the City of Eisleben

Cannonballs
Iron, 16th century
Diameter 80 mm, 90 mm
On loan from the City of Eisleben

Lansquenet and wife
Daniel Hopfer
Etching, reprint from the original plate, 16th/17th
century
203 mm x 148 mm (219 mm x 167 mm)
Classification number: fl XX 8815

Martin Luther
Worldly Authority and the Limits to Obedience
(Von weltlicher Oberkeit, wie weit man ihr
Gehorsam schuldig sei)
Wittenberg: Nickel Schirlentz, 1523
Classification number: Kn K 34
Benzing 1509, VD 16 L 7316, WA 11. 230 Ab

Martin Luther
Admonition of Peace on the Twelve Articles of
the Swabian Peasants. Also Against the Murderous and Thieving Hordes of Peasants (Ermahnung zum Frieden auf die zwölf Artikel der Bauernschaft in Schwaben. Auch wider die räuberischen und mörderischen Rotten der anderen
Bauern)
Wittenberg: Josef Klug, 1525
Classification number: Ag 4° 206 r
Benzing 2119, VD 16 L 4692, WA 18. 282 C u. 18.
345 A

John the Steadfast, Prince Elector of Saxony
Lucas Cranach the Elder (workshop)
Oil on beech, 16th century
495 mm x 358 mm (601 mm x 464 mm)
Classification number: G 88

John Frederick the Magnanimous, Prince Elec-
tor of Saxony
Monogram master IS (Cranach workshop)
Oil on beech, 16th century
495 mm x 360 mm (600 mm x 463 mm)
Classification number: G 91

Sword
Wrought iron and steel, turned wood, 16th century
1,055 mm x 290 mm x 70 mm
Classification number: MH K 220

Large Lecture Hall

Disputation lectern
Johann Jacob Marchand
Wood, gold leaf and paint on kaolin and chalk
ground, front and back panels with acanthus
carvings and painted medallions, 1685
3,750 mm x 4,360 mm x 1,400 mm
Classification number: K 17

Frederick III the Wise, Prince Elector of Saxony
Lucas Cranach the Younger
Oil on canvas, c. 1570
2,220 mm x 1,070 mm (2,430 mm x 1,280 mm)
On loan from the Wittenberg Preachers Seminary

Duke Maurice, Prince Elector of Saxony
Lucas Cranach the Younger
Oil on canvas, c. 1570
2,170 mm x 1,060 mm
On loan from the Wittenberg Preachers Seminary

Martin Pollich von Mellerstadt
Oil on limewood, c. 1608
860 mm x 580 mm (980 mm x 670 mm)
On loan from the Wittenberg Preachers Seminary

Andreas Schato
Oil on canvas
940 mm x 770 mm
On loan from the Wittenberg Preachers Seminary

Joachim von Beust
Oil on canvas
925 mm x 690 mm (1,040 mm x 815 mm)
Classification number: G 145

Abraham Calov
Oil on canvas
930 mm x 760 mm
On loan from the Wittenberg Preachers Seminary

Flag of Wittenberg University
Gouache on silk appliquéd to silk, silk fringe
border, double eagle, with the coat of arms of
the electorate of Saxony and the elector's coro-
net applied in the round section
16th century
1,000 mm x 1,120 mm
On loan from the Wittenberg Preachers Seminary

Johannes Meisner
Oil on canvas
930 mm x 740 mm
On loan from the Wittenberg Preachers Seminary

Johann Andreas Quenstedt
Oil on canvas
940 mm x 750 mm
On loan from the Wittenberg Preachers Seminary

Gottfried Suevus II
Michael Adolph Siebenhaar
Oil on canvas, 1717
920 mm x 720 mm
On loan from the Wittenberg Preachers Seminary

Flag of the Faculty of Philosophy
Colored silk embroidery, appliquéd to silk, silk
fringe border. Patron Saint Catherine of Alexand-
ria in the round section is accompanied by her
attributes of sword, wheel and book. 16th century
1,000 mm x 1,280 mm
On loan from the Wittenberg Preachers Seminary

Kaspar Ziegler
Oil on canvas
910 mm x 710 mm
On loan from the Wittenberg Preachers Seminary

Johann Deutschmann
Oil on canvas
980 mm x 740 mm
On loan from the Wittenberg Preachers Seminary

Martin Chladenius
Oil on canvas
870 mm x 680 mm
On loan from the Wittenberg Preachers Seminary

Flag of the Hungarian students' association
Gouache on silk, silver paillette lettering, Hungarian coat of arms with crown of St. Stephen,
16th century
860 mm x 1,460 mm
On loan from the Wittenberg Preachers Seminary

Georg Wilhelm Kirchmair
Michael Adolph Siebenhaar
Oil on canvas, 1728
910 mm x 740 mm
On loan from the Wittenberg Preachers Seminary

Johann Heinrich von Berger
Oil on canvas
870 mm x 680 mm
On loan from the Wittenberg Preachers Seminary

Christian I, Prince Elector of Saxony
Zacharias Wehme
Oil on canvas, 1605
2,200 mm x 1,050 mm
On loan from the Wittenberg Preachers Seminary

August I, Prince Elector of Saxony
Lucas Cranach the Younger
Oil on canvas, c. 1570
2,160 mm x 1,050 mm (2,300 mm x 1,270 mm)
On loan from the Wittenberg Preachers Seminary

Marriage and Family, 1526–1546

Rosary
Turned wood, cord, 16th century
460 mm
Classification number: K 2

Martin Luther
Why Nuns Should Leave Convents as a Matter
of Faith (Ursache und Antwort, dass Jungfrauen
Klöster göttlich verlassen mögen)
Wittenberg: Lucas Cranach and Christian
Döring, 1523, first edition
Classification number: Ag 4° 198 Theta
Benzing 1561, VD 16 L 6888, WA 11. 389 A

Martin Luther
On Married Life (Vom ehelichen Leben)
Augsburg: Heinrich Steiner, 1523
Classification number: Ag 4° 198 f
Benzing 1250, VD 16 L 7034, WA 10,2. 270 L

Martin Luther
Lucas Cranach the Elder
Parchment/paper on beech, 1525
Diameter 110 mm (217 mm x 219 mm)
Classification number: G 11

Martin Luther
Lucas Cranach the Elder (workshop)
Oil on beech, 1528
358 mm x 257 mm (418 mm x 317 mm)
Classification number: G 16

Katharina von Bora
Lucas Cranach the Elder (workshop)
Oil on beech, 1528
360 mm x 260 mm (457 mm x 348 mm)
Classification number: G 17

Wedding goblet for Luther and his wife
Gilt silver, 1525
501 mm x 165 mm
On loan from the City of Wittenberg

Wall closets
Pine, 16th century
Eastern closet:
1,560 mm x 1,107 mm x 567 mm
Western closet:
1,562 mm x 1,092 mm x 555 mm

Katharina von Bora
after Hans Brosamer
Woodcut, after 1530
179 mm x 242 mm (346 mm x 276 mm)
Classification number: grfl III 953

Clock
Germany
Iron, first half of the 16th century
480 mm x 220 mm x 220 mm
Classification number: K 305

Padlock
Germany
Wrought iron, c. 1500
63 mm x 42 mm x 22 mm
Classification number: K 304

Knife for self-defense
Switzerland or Southern Germany

Wrought iron, stag horn
Early 16th century
397 mm x 38 mm x 24 mm
Classification number: K 280

Casket
Nuremberg
Sheet iron, etched, 16th century
120 mm x 184 mm x 106 mm
Classification number: K 279

Electorate of Saxony and Duchy of Saxony
Frederick III the Wise, Albrecht, and designated
Elector John
"Schreckenberger" or "Engelgroschen" coin, no
year (1498–1500)
Annaberg mint
Mintmaster Heinrich Stein and Augustin Horn
Silver, 29 mm, 4.0 g
Classification number: MH M 898b
Krug 2140

Electorate of Saxony and Duchy of Saxony
Frederick III the Wise, designated Elector John
the Steadfast, and Duke George
"Zinsgroschen" coin, no year (1508–25)
Buchholz mint
Silver, 27 mm, 2.4 g
Classification number: MH M 54
Götz 4248

Electorate of Saxony and Duchy of Saxony
John the Steadfast and Duke George
Thaler, no year (1525–30)
Annaberg mint
Mintmaster Melchior Irmisch
Silver, 38 mm, 28.8 g
Classification number: M 87
Schulten 3040, Schnee 51

George the Bearded, Duchy of Saxony
Thaler, 1531
Freiberg mint
Mintmaster Hans Hausmann
Silver, 38 mm, 28.0 g
Classification number: M 50
Schulten 3213, Schnee 667

Electorate of Saxony and Duchy of Saxony
John Frederick the Magnanimous and Duke
George
Thaler, 1535
Schneeberg mint
Mintmaster Sebastian Funcke
Silver, 39 mm, 29.0 g
Classification number: M 71
Schulten 3063, Schnee 74

Candlestick
Earthenware, 16th century
265 mm x 105 mm
On loan from the City of Eisleben

Three-legged pipkin
Earthenware, 16th century
130 mm x 115 mm x 140 mm
On loan from the City of Eisleben

Rounded jar
Earthenware, 16th century
105 mm x 130 mm x 110 mm
On loan from the City of Eisleben

Bowl with handle
Earthenware, 16th century
80 mm x 175 mm x 155 mm
On loan from the City of Eisleben

Pitcher
Earthenware, 16th century
165 mm x 155 mm x 125 mm
On loan from the City of Eisleben

Lantern
Oak, fir, iron, glass, 16th century
225 mm x 103 mm x 110 mm
Classification number: K 288

Round brass platter
Nuremberg
Brass, hammered, early 16th century
Diameter 450 mm
Classification number: K 273

Aquamanile
Cast brass, 16th century
165 mm x 77 mm x 170 mm
Classification number: MH K 75

Candlestick
Cast brass, c. 1600
110 mm x 100 mm
Classification number: K 278

Three-legged pipkin
Bronze, 16th/17th century
255 mm x 330 mm x 290 mm
Classification number: K 291

Mortar and pestle
Southern Europe
Cast brass, first half of the 16th century
113 mm x 122 mm (mortar)
172 mm x 32 mm (pestle)
Classification number: K 302

Picture of a girl
after Lucas Cranach the Elder, 1520
Oil on beech, 16th century (copy)
368 mm x 265 mm (473 mm x 370 mm)
Classification number: G 12

Deed of sale of Luther's house to the university
by his sons for 3,700 florins
Parchment, Wittenberg, September 27, 1564
410 mm x 480 mm
Classification number: Urk./857

Luther's Friends

Luther's tankard
Turned root wood, first half of the 16th century
Silver mounting, 1694
155 mm x 112 mm
Classification number: K 4a

Martin Luther
Lucas Cranach the Elder (workshop)
Oil on beech, 1540
202 mm x 144 mm (330 mm x 275 mm)
Classification number: G 70

Philipp Melanchthon
Lucas Cranach the Elder (workshop)
Oil on beech, 1540
203 mm x 145 mm (264 mm x 204 mm)
Classification number: G 71

Johannes Bugenhagen
Lucas Cranach the Elder
Oil on beech, 1537
361 mm x 235 mm (453 mm x 333 mm)
On loan from the Wittenberg Preachers Seminary

Table Talk (Colloquia oder Tischreden Doctor
Martini Lutheri)